SERVANTS OF THE LIVING GOD

SERVANTS OF THE LIVING GOD

Anglican clergy tell of the impact of the Holy Spirit on their lives and ministries

Edited by
Peter and Jane Byron-Davies

Terra Nova Publications

Published in Great Britain by
Terra Nova Publications Ltd
PO Box 2400
Bradford on Avon, Wiltshire BA15 2YN

ISBN 1 901949 04 4

Cover design: Gazelle Creative Productions
Cover printed by The Shires Press, Trowbridge, Wiltshire

Printed in Great Britain at
The Cromwell Press, Trowbridge, Wiltshire

Contents

Acknowledgements

The publishers and editors acknowledge with warm appreciation the kindness of Bishop David Pytches.

We are grateful to Tony Collins, and Monarch Publications, publishers of John Woolmer's book *Healing and Deliverance* (1999), for assistance received.

Thanks are expressed to Kingsway Publications, for permission to quote from *Nine O'Clock in the Morning* by Dennis Bennett.

Last but not least, our thanks are due to the contributors, who have so openly and honestly written about their experiences, in order to encourage those who are seeking more of the love and power of the Holy Spirit, who always glorifies Jesus.

Foreword

Servants of the Living God is a book about people and God. Ever since I first heard my father tell of a powerful spiritual experience, during the mini-revival in Lowestoft in 1922, which changed his life as the then Rector of Pettaugh in Suffolk, and later read *From Death unto Life* by William Haslam, the Rector of Baldhu, Cornwall, I have always been fascinated by other people's experiences of God.

How many people were gripped by the opening chapter of Dennis Bennett's book *Nine O'Clock in the Morning* where a young Anglican priest comes round to Bennett's house to discuss his worries about a lay couple in his church?

> *'They've really got me going!' he said.*
> *'Whatever are you talking about?' Bennett asked.*
> *'Well they come to church all the time—they hardly ever came until five months ago—now they are just there...looking happy.'*
> *'Looking happy in church? —That is suspicious behaviour!' said Bennett.*
> *'Yes, but—well, the thing that bothers me most is that when I asked them how come they turn up all the time and look so happy, they said, "We've been baptised in the Holy Spirit!"'*
> *'They've been what in what?' Bennett asked.*

Whatever the correct theological terminology for their experience of God might be—there were still other good things about them that the young priest wanted to share. This couple readily volunteered to help in any way they could in the church, whilst they tithed ten per cent of their income to its funds. Such a report was enough to provoke an investigation by Dennis Bennett, the Episcopal Rector in Van Nuys, California, whose own story was soon after to make the cover page of *Time* magazine, telling of his commitment to renewal in the Holy Spirit.

For too many years the Holy Spirit has been regarded as the Cinderella of the Trinity, and the displaced Person of the godhead. He is in reality 'The Lord and Giver of Life', the Divine Executive and Change Agent of the Holy Trinity. He is the dynamically invasive presence of God in the world. But how many clergy have assumed what Dr. Jim Packer once described as 'a paralytic traditionalism' —we have never changed and we never will; a 'pharisaic formalism' —outward correctness being the thing; or 'a naturalistic Pelagian moralism' —never mind this regeneration or renewal stuff, it's our good works which will get us to heaven? Too often, they are totally unaware of the 'available presence' of the Holy Spirit.

In this new book *Servants of the Living God*, eight Anglican clergy have been re-discovering something of their life-changing experiences and the fuller implications of this for themselves and their ministries. These 'servants of the living God' hold to the orthodox Christian faith and have been significantly impacted by the Holy Spirit. Their book says what Catherine Marshall was saying, some years ago, in her bestselling book *Something More*.

The Christian life is a pilgrimage full of new touches of God—some in the valley and some on the mountain top. Who knows when or where? There has to be some mystery about God and there is always a surprise factor in the Christian life, as C.S. Lewis shows in his book *Surprised by Joy*. Some find other people's experiences of God rather threatening. This could well be so if we are made to feel we must all have exactly the same experiences before we can move along in our own Christian journey. But this book avoids all that.

There was a time when I might have simply written off people who had experiences which had not been mine. We tend to see ourselves as the norm. They are probably slightly mad or at least odd—or over the top! By not valuing what they were telling me, I might well have quenched the Spirit in them and myself, demeaned their experience of God and belittled their particular touch of Glory.

Learning of the walk of others, as *Servants of the Living God* invites us to do, opens up whole new vistas of possibility for us, though God, of course, has no *clone* disciples and, as the book illustrates, He does not touch us all in precisely the same way with exactly the same effect. Through these pages the Lord excites us with wonder at His mercy and encourages us with hope by His boundless grace. Certainly He has something more for all of us.

These men write very simply and honestly. There is nothing glib about their accounts. They do not push us too hard, preach too long or promise too much. They write humbly revealing their own hearts and the realities of life in the parish. We need these records. The heritage of the whole Church is the whole heritage of the Church. Their heritage is our heritage. This is the kind of book which encourages those 'whose hearts are set on pilgrimage' not to give up! There is always something more—He gives more grace—grace upon grace. It is never exhausted. He pours out His Spirit without limit. We should never think that we have had our full ration.

I believe this book will also encourage those who have been on the road some time, those 'who have borne the heat and burden of the day', who may even have become a little cynical. I was delightfully challenged recently when talking to a surgeon who was with the great divine, Martin Lloyd Jones, as he lay dying, a few years back. Martin said to his doctor, 'You may give me something for the pain, but not if it will stop me seeing the glory! Don't stop me seeing the glory!' He was certainly expecting more, right up to the end—which would really be a new beginning for him.

In fact, a touch of God's glory is usually a new beginning for all of us. That is my prayer for every reader of these testimonies whose 'heart and flesh cry out for the living God'—for encouragement, assurance, comfort, refreshing, anointing, guidance—whatever. I congratulate Peter and Jane Byron-Davies for getting these contributions together. It is a privilege to commend this lovely, very readable, little book.

David Pytches

'Doing the Stuff'

PETER H. LAWRENCE

Team Rector of Canford Magna, Dorset
and Chairman of the Renewal Group in the Salisbury Diocese
A well-known Christian speaker and writer, his publications include
The Hot Line, Christian Healing and
Doing What Comes Supernaturally (Terra Nova)

I always knew it was in the book. I always believed that Jesus proclaimed the kingdom, healed the sick and cast out demons. I always believed that Peter, Stephen, Philip and Paul (as recorded in the Acts of the Apostles) really did do what Jesus did. I even believed the Christian books I read about other people at other times and in other places doing the same. I guess Smith Wigglesworth has always been something of a hero of mine. It was just that I never believed I could do it even though I always wanted to try.

It was not the excitement of signs and wonders, miracle conversions, bright lights or fame and fortune which attracted me. Perhaps that is why I so admired down-to-earth Smith, the Bradford plumber. It was the truth of biblical Christianity which drew me. It can be very embarrassing explaining to people how the Bible really is true, it's just that these things don't happen today. It was never easy saying God spoke directly to people for several thousand years but since He's had a book out He's been taking a long vacation. I have frequently found it painful to look at the physical sufferings of very dear friends and say, 'I have nothing to offer' when, deep down inside, the Spirit who raised Jesus from the dead was supposed to be residing in my life.

My desire and search for true Bible-based Christianity regularly ran aground on two particularly large rocks. The first one was experience. I had never been nurtured or taught any practical ways of tapping into God's supernatural love and power. One Nottingham vicar was very helpful to me as a theological student at least in keeping the desire and hope alive within me. He held a well-attended healing service at which a few people were healed, and held a prayer meeting at which people did speak in tongues. It provided a glimpse of the unseen world and confirmed my belief in the reality of it all, but there was not the time to ask how and what and why. There was nobody available to show me where to lay my hands, what to pray, what to think and feel and say. They did not teach us how to heal the sick or hear God speaking at theological college; consequently, when I left to do my curacy I knew as little and as much as those around me and we made no headway.

The second rock which capsized my weak efforts was theology. I have always been all too painfully aware that the main-line Christian churches who experience most 'signs and wonders' believe different things from me, and this really halted my own individual progress. I read much of their literature; believed at least a good half of their stories, but found I could swallow very little of their so-called biblical theology. I was no expert at all on healing or signs and wonders, but I did know the Bible. There were two main problems.

1. The Baptism in the Holy Spirit.

I was told that conversion was a two stage process. You got saved and then some time later—maybe a day, a week or even a year—you got the Baptism in the Holy Spirit. The sign that this second stage had occurred was receiving the gift of speaking in tongues.

Surprisingly, my own experience could be seen to fit this theology. I was very definitely saved when I was fourteen. I repented of my sins, believed in the Lord Jesus Christ and asked him to be my Lord and Saviour. I began speaking in tongues for the first time when I was twenty two. It looks as though this was a long time and a rather large gap, but considering I belonged to a church which taught us how spiritual gifts died out with the Apostles it wasn't bad.

The 'Baptism in the Holy Spirit' fitted my experience but it didn't fit my Bible. I found no such *thing* as, 'the Baptism in the Holy Spirit' in the New Testament. Jesus is the Baptiser in the Holy Spirit. Being *baptised*—immersed, soaked—in the Holy Spirit is an activity which occurs again and again. It is never a noun—always a verb. When do you get the 'second blessing'? Believers in the New Testament seemed to get it between the first and the third, with the first definitely coming at conversion.

'...if anyone does not have the Spirit of Christ, he does not belong to Christ' (Romans 8:9).

To become a Christian is to be 'born of the Spirit' (John 3:8).

'If anyone acknowledges that Jesus is the Son of God, God lives in him and he in God' (1 John 4:15).

When we become Christians we receive the Holy Spirit. What seems to happen when we speak in tongues, exercise other gifts or flap up and down like a chicken is that the Holy Spirit comes on us, and fills us, again and again. This is the teaching of Paul's letter to the Ephesian Christians who had been saved and baptised in the Holy Spirit when they believed (Ephesians 1:13,14). He tells them to 'be filled with the Spirit' (Ephesians 5:18) and the Greek means 'to go on being filled'.

To my mind, the problem arose from an attempt to systematise God and make doctrines out of description rather than prescription.

John 3:1–21 is clear 'prescriptive' teaching.

'...no one can see the kingdom of God unless he is born again' (John 3:3).

'...no one can enter the kingdom of God unless he is born of water and the Spirit' (John 3:5).

'So it is with everyone born of the Spirit' (John 3:8).

'...everyone who believes in him may have eternal life' (John 3:15).

'...whoever believes in him shall not perish but have eternal life' (John 3:16).

'Whoever believes in him is not condemned' (John 3:18).

The 'no-ones', 'everyones' and 'whoevers' go with Paul's 'anyone' (Romans 8:9) and John's 'anyone' (1 John 4:15) already mentioned. This is eternal truth prescribed for all people at all times in all circumstances.

But the Acts of the Apostles is basically 'description' or testimony. Luke describes what happened to different people in different places at different times, and no two experiences are identical. So, in Acts 2 the Apostles are filled with the Spirit and speak in other known languages. But—they have already proclaimed the Kingdom, healed the sick and cast out demons with the power and authority of Jesus in Luke Chapter 9, and received the Holy Spirit in John Chapter 20, prior to Jesus' ascension. The Samaritans believe (Acts 8), are baptised in water and then receive the Holy Spirit when Peter and John lay hands on them. No mention of tongues. After Paul's Damascus Road experience (Chapter 9), Paul receives the laying-on-of-hands, receives his sight and is filled with the Holy Spirit. Then he is baptised in water. Cornelius and friends believe (Chapter 10), the Holy Spirit comes on them and they speak in tongues without the laying-on-of-hands. Then they are water-baptised. The Ephesians believe (Chapter 19), are baptised, and when Paul places his hands on them the Holy Spirit comes on them and they speak in tongues and prophesy.

A variety of experiences are described by Luke. 'Received', 'filled', 'came on' seem to be interchangeable. Language about the invisible God is very difficult anyway. Sometimes tongues are mentioned—sometimes not. Sometimes people are baptised in water first—sometimes afterwards. Sometimes they receive the laying-on-of-hands—sometimes not. 'The Baptism in the Holy Spirit' is not mentioned, but it seems right to say all of these are examples of Jesus baptising them, immersing them, again and again, in the Holy Spirit (cf. Acts 1:5, 2:33). Even so, trying to make a doctrine out of described experience rather than prescribed truth—particularly when all the experiences are slightly different—has never seemed to me to be sound biblical procedure.

All a bit pedantic—a bit nit-picking and niggling—BUT, it was where it led that made me struggle. If you do not speak in tongues you are a second class Christian—or maybe not even one at all. That was my stumbling block, even though I did.

2. Healing as a Covenant Right

The material I read about healing always seemed to link being healed directly with what Jesus did at Calvary. Everyone was then encouraged to claim their healing as a Covenant right. Sadly, I could not find that in the Bible either. My New Testament does not teach that Jesus died for my sins and my sicknesses. 1 Peter, which is often quoted, is all about spiritual healing—forgiveness of sins—not physical healing. Anyway, to die for sickness makes no sense. I could find no biblical justification for seeing physical healing as a covenant right due to Calvary—and I could never tolerate the idea of shouting at people in wheelchairs telling them to have more faith. That has always seemed more like abuse to me than healing. The New Testaments on my shelf link healing directly to the work of the Holy Spirit—not the cross.

The teaching I read on healing and the Baptism in the Holy Spirit didn't seem to match the New Testament, and the style of many healing evangelists did not seem to match the way Jesus did healing. No-one to teach me. No theology to satisfy me. On these two rocks my personal search for an experience of true biblical Christianity ran aground. That was when John Wimber came along.

John obviously believed every Christian received the Holy Spirit at conversion. That fitted my Bible and my experience. There were certainly times between the ages of fourteen and twenty two (being saved and speaking in tongues), when God came powerfully on me. Most of them occurred during worship when God's love was so close and so tangible I longed for the nearer presence of heaven. I am convinced the Holy Spirit was in my life from the moment I was converted.

John Wimber ministered very effectively using 'words of knowledge'; spiritual gifts given by God through the Holy Spirit. Going where led: praying where and how led; seeing people genuinely healed. No promise of healing. No shouting. No hype or emotionalism. Listening to God and inviting Him to take the initiative. It fitted the Jesus who only did what he saw the Father doing (John 5:19) perfectly. Healing was definitely linked to the work of the Holy Spirit rather than the cross. Just as in the New Testament.

The way—the method—the door to all John Wimber did in the name of Jesus, was to ask God to send His Holy Spirit again and again. I re-read Luke 11:1–13 with renewed vigour. The Asking—and go on asking; Seeking—and go on seeking; Knocking—and go on knocking (Luke 11:9) fitted Paul's 'be filled'—and go on being filled (Ephesians 5:18).

The feeding of a son with a fish or an egg (Luke 11:11) matched the 'daily bread' of verse 3. You do not feed children just once or twice in a lifetime but again and again.

And Jesus' declaration 'how much more will your Father in heaven give the Holy Spirit to those who ask him' (Luke 11:13) said to me that God will always send the Holy Spirit, again and again, to His children who ask Him through Jesus. The problem of why ask Him to come when He is already here caused me no problems, having studied theology and religious language at university. God is not like limited finite human beings. People come and go. God comes and comes.

I was satisfied; excited and frightened; hopeful and fearful; but satisfied. It was biblically OK to ask God to send His Holy Spirit again and again. So I did. It changed my life. We got people saved. We got people healed. We got people delivered. And we got crucified.

It was not an instant 'success'. I asked God to send His Holy Spirit on our congregation in church services and on smaller housegroups during the week and at first very little happened. After the stories I told them about the John Wimber conference, I think most people were relieved. But they humoured me, loved me and went along with whatever I suggested until, gradually, a few manifestations began to occur.

A bald head heated up like a stove during ministry and its owner felt the strain and stress of a busy day drain away. Several people began to speak in tongues for the first time. Quite specific 'words' were received, given and claimed. Some aches and pains were eased.

Spasmodically, more dramatic things began to take place. A 'word' about a ventricle with ensuing ministry brought quite a dramatic healing to a heart problem as much pain and pounding palpitations stopped instantly at the laying-on-of-hands. Our churchwarden fell over in the Spirit and was instantly and permanently healed of trapped sciatic nerves and torn muscles. Sister Mary, a seventy four year old Church of England Penguin, shook violently, received a physical healing and was released into the gift of speaking in tongues. Reports began to come in weekly of others who were being profoundly helped when members of our newly formed ministry teams asked God to send His Holy Spirit. And then it happened....

One Sunday morning, I invited everyone at the main service to stand while I asked God to send His Holy Spirit upon them. Instantly, a lady fell over sideways knocking three other ladies flying. Some of them received bruising and all of them a degree of fear. One just about coped. One switched to the early morning service and one never came again. We had not expected it, we were not prepared and we did not handle it well.

There were several unhappy bunnies who did not want this Holy Spirit stuff any more and a general meeting was called. Some of us prayed like mad beforehand. Grievances were heard—anxieties expressed—and then the testimonies began.

The churchwarden had lived beside the church for fifty years. He was now sixty five. Well-known. Well-liked. After three months of so much pain that he could not sit, stand or lie down without discomfort —three months of not being able to dress himself—he had fallen over in the power of the Holy Spirit, and had been completely healed. He has been digging the church gardens on a regular basis ever since.

Sister Mary was greatly loved and deeply respected by everyone in our congregation. All her life she had been searching for spiritual gifts—

18

the power to heal—the closeness and intimacy of God. Now she was beginning to find them.

Another lady, well into her seventies, did much for the church and unknown to many she had suffered considerably at the hands of others in her earlier years. The Spirit came powerfully on her and she fell back into her seat. In the space of minutes God took away years of hurt and pain. 'It was wonderful', she kept saying. And now, totally set free to forgive, she felt like a new creation.

A churchwarden; a sister from the nursing community of St. John the Divine; an elderly, hard-working pillar of society—all shared their stories and in the end there was nowhere for the critics to go. These elderly, much loved, deeply respected saints ended the debate. We had lessons to learn, but the ministry was allowed to continue.

We learned not to ask God to come in the service before the anthem. The choir practised hard, but they were unable to minister in song one day, being sprawled out on the chancel steps under the power of God.

We learned to ask God to come at the end of the service, when everyone else had done their bit first. An unbelieving policeman came in, stood up, fell down, got up again and went out as a believer. He became the new churchwarden. The husband of a believer was brought to church and braved the ministry. He heated up, shook all over, crashed down, slid around on the floor and accepted Jesus as his Lord and Saviour.

I saw people healed before my eyes. The Spirit came on a man who was virtually deaf. He wept for half-an-hour as the Lord revealed to him the sins in his life. Afterwards he removed his large hearing aids and could hear clearly without them for the first time in years.

A lady had been chronically ill for twenty years with stomach pain. The hospital could not find the problem. When the Spirit came on her she realised there were two people she needed to forgive. After this and the laying-on-of hands the pain went. On examination at the hospital plus new X-rays it was discovered that her curvature of the spine was now healed. (We didn't know she had this problem and did not pray for it). The X-rays also showed the source of the stomach pain, which had been obscured previously by the curved spine. The stomach problem was then cured easily by surgery.

A lady with painful arthritis experienced the love of God coming all over her as she was filled with the Spirit. God told her to go and forgive her mother. As she did this the arthritis left her from head to toe. This was subsequently confirmed by the medical profession.

I asked God to send His Holy Spirit at a celebration one Saturday night. A lady on the back row fell over on the pew and lay there untroubled for an hour. It was obvious to sensitive onlookers that something deep and powerful was going on. She had cancer. The surgeon examined her the following Tuesday. 'Good Lord!' he exclaimed. 'Yes he is, isn't he?' replied the lady. She was healed, and no longer needed an operation.

But the one I shall never forget was the sixteen year old boy who was virtually blind. He could barely see a metre. As I asked God to send His Holy Spirit upon him, his face twisted and sneered malevolently, his body became tense and a foul-sounding language came out of his mouth. 'In the name of Jesus,' I said firmly, 'I command you to come out of him. Go to Jesus and never return.' There was a struggle within him. The tension appeared to rise up from his stomach to his throat before it was suddenly released with a loud cough. Peace came all over him. He opened his eyes and in amazement began to describe things he could see on the furthest horizon. To God be all the glory.

At times I've had to take a fair amount of flack from Christians of all denominations. Other clergy, especially the hierarchy, treat me with caution. I don't get many invitations to minister in traditional churches. Many try to pour doubt and scorn upon me—but—I was there. I have seen these things. Repeatedly, the Bible came to life right in front of me. Whatever men may say or do, I can never be the same again.

Sad to say, wonderful healings do not happen all the time, and I have taken some very tragic funerals during this same period. I pray for many people who are not healed, though many do receive God's blessing in one way or another. We can only do what the Father is doing. We may miss it more times than we spot it, but the times when we ask God the Father through Jesus to send His Holy Spirit are the ones when we seem to spot it most.

And yet—one further thing saddens me even more. In the fifteen years since I attended my first Wimber conference at Sheffield, I have met many clergy and leaders who were also there.

'What did you think of the conference?' I ask.

'Marvellous,' they often reply. 'Enjoyed every minute of it.'

'What did you think of the teaching?' I continue.

'Fine,' they respond. 'It is so good to have some sensible, biblical teaching on the kingdom, the Spirit and healing.'

'And what did you think of the ministry?' I enquire.

'Amazing. Sensitive. Loving. Gentle. Just like Jesus and his disciples in Bible times. I saw people saved, healed and set free from demons.'

With very few exceptions this pattern is repeated over and over. Many clergy and leaders really do believe it is just that.... My final question is usually the one which brings a sad reply.

'How are you getting on doing it in your own church?' I try to ask with a gentle, hopeful smile.

'Ah well! Yes. Good question,' they often begin; trying to stall for time. 'Our people don't seem to be quite ready for it yet. Not quite America is it? We do pray for people occasionally, in the side chapel or in house groups... but....' and most of them move away sheepishly, hoping to find a more comfortable person to engage in conversation.

I do understand where they are coming from. Despite all God has graciously allowed me to see and experience I don't find it easy myself. Now I am over fifty, the days are getting longer while the years are getting shorter. Risk-taking is not a natural gift which comes with grey hair. It is far less hassle looking backwards from a rocking chair than forwards. Time is drifting by and the full gospel of Jesus Christ all too easily gets pushed to the sidelines, the margins, the fringes, even the gutter, as I naturally search for greater personal comfort.

Our national pastime of knocking the guy in charge doesn't encourage much risk-taking among leaders. Perhaps we are getting the leaders and the churches we deserve. The struggle presents itself more like a heavy cross than a light yoke. In Church life it is much easier making room for those who want to play at being God than inviting the one who does it best to play Himself. God doesn't moan and groan like they do. He never barges in or forces Himself upon us.

But, deep inside, something or someone reminds me I have but one life to live and that will soon be over. The young Evan Roberts dared to ask God to send His Holy Spirit again and again, and the Welsh Revival of 1904 saw 100,000 souls led to Christ. That is a truth which challenges my complacency. Dare I recapture the zeal and honesty of youth—my first love?

The stakes we are playing for are very high. While the rest of the world is experiencing revival, the Church in England is declining in numbers. The choice to leave God out of Church on a Sunday is not one that sits comfortably with me. However difficult I may find it at times, I don't ever want to go back to life without His Spirit. The more pleasant-sounding options don't make life any easier on the inside once true biblical Christianity has been tasted.

I have been changed, I am being changed, but my deepest prayer is that I will go on being changed. Today there are just as many hurts and pains in unfulfilled lives around me as ever there were and it seems churlish indeed to consider my own creature comforts first. My flesh is weak, but in my spirit I want more of Him—more love; more power to do the things He did and does and wants to do—for others' sakes and for His name's sake. Logically it can only be crazy to try and achieve this in my own strength. The only way I know how to begin obtaining such desires is to ask God the Father through Jesus to send His Holy Spirit on us, again and again. This is what changed me, this is what is changing me, and by the grace of God this is what will go on changing me if I can find the courage and boldness to do it and go on doing it.

God Knew Best

JOHN WOOLMER

Rector of Shepton Mallet, Somerset
and author of a number of books, including
'Thinking Clearly about Prayer' and
'Thinking Clearly about Healing and Deliverance' (Monarch)

GOD'S PATIENT CALL

'Colonel Sandford, if you can't read the lessons better than that, you'd better cease.' The booming voice of Lady Carden, the squire's wife, rang out across the churchyard of St. Martin's, East Woodhay. The Colonel gave up and I, at the age of fourteen, became one of his replacements. So began my first unexpected experience of Anglican ministry, in the little village church to which my mother had taken me since I was about three. Lesson reading was not always a success. At public school, I convulsed my friends when I innocently read Acts chapter eight as Philip's encounter with the Ethiopian 'unch' (eunuch).

Reading for my degree in Mathematics at Oxford, I felt that I 'ought' to continue going to church. I was recommended to try St. Aldate's. It was impressive to see a church so full that people were sitting on the window sills. I heard the gospel preached—especially by Cuthbert Bardsley, then Bishop of Coventry. I did not feel that I needed conversion, and my village rector agreed! In my last term, I heard Ernest Shippam of Shippam's paste, telling how he had been converted at Harringay through Billy Graham's preaching. He talked about how this experience had brought his religious upbringing alive, and how it had transformed his relationship with his workforce and with his family. I was deeply moved. I had never before heard anyone speak of how God could alter their day to day life. Ernest invited people to come forward, after the service, to pray with him. I made rapidly for the door, but I could not get out. Sheepishly, I made my way forward, and talked to Ernest. That afternoon, I made a simple prayer of commitment to Christ, and joined St. Aldate's beginners' group. It was the start of a significant friendship with the vicar, Canon Keith de Berry.

In September, I began a temporary teaching job at Winchester College. Appointed for one year, I stayed nearly twelve! Arriving with great evangelical visions for the conversion of the school, I was quickly disillusioned. At the end of my first term, I was sitting beside the captain of the house in which I was lunching. He turned to me and said, 'Sir, why should four hundred atheists go and sing *Hark, the Herald Angels* in the cathedral this afternoon?' I could think of no good answer.

Over the next few years I started training as a Reader. I went on holidays with St. Aldate's, and began to read Christian books. *The Cross and the Switchblade*, which I used to adapt for weekday services in the Junior Chapel, was particularly influential. It raised, very sharply, the question, 'how does God speak to us today?'

GOD'S MORE URGENT CALL

I wanted to start a Bible study group, but did not know how to begin. I felt the Holy Spirit say, 'Go to the early morning service tomorrow, and a particular boy (Tom) will be there. You are to ask him.... He will be the cornerstone of this new group.' The next morning I woke up just five minutes before the 7.30 service was due to start. 'Sorry, Lord, I've missed it!' Something propelled me out of bed. Somewhat breathless, I arrived late for the service in the mediaeval Chantry. About twenty people were present—members of staff, leavers, and Tom. My heart leapt, and a small Bible study group was duly formed. The main result was that I became more open to listening to God. I was already trying to sort out the question of offering myself for ordination. I was under quite a lot of pressure from Keith de Berry, who was gently upbraided by my headmaster for trying to remove a member of his staff! After about a year of inconclusive prayer, I said to the Lord, 'You'd better make it clear!'

Another St. Aldate's holiday came round. I met a delightful young lady. Unattached at the age of 25, I was beginning to feel the need for a relationship. She seemed attracted, but also cautious. In the middle of a two week holiday, I discovered the reason. She had just got engaged! That night, I prayed very hard. The Lord seemed to say three things. First: she is not the right girl; back off. Secondly, while you are giving things up, give up your career and follow my way. Thirdly, read Psalm 143, verse 8. As I did so, the words 'Let me hear of your loving kindness in the morning' leapt off the page.

The next day, Sunday August 6th (the Feast of the Transfiguration) sealed everything. I went to Ambleside Parish Church. Keith, from whom I had carefully hidden my struggle of the last year, was preaching. We sang Psalm 143 ('probability 1/150', said my mathematical mind.) My spiritual pulse raced. Keith preached a simple biblical sermon, which included the words, 'When Jesus came down the mountain, humanly speaking he could return to Galilee as a fairly successful minor prophet, or he could do what God really was calling him to do.' Then he paused and turned to us. 'Some of you, in a lesser way, are in the same situation. You can stay where you are, or follow the new way which God is really calling you to take!'

There was no way out. I had asked for a sign and had been given one. The previous night could have been just emotionalism. The psalm could have been a coincidence. The preaching could have been for someone else. But all three combined with devastating power.

Two years later, still somewhat reluctantly, I arrived at Westcott Theological College, on what was called a schoolmaster's ordination course. It was to last over a series of long vacation terms. My life was in turmoil. My mother had just died. My father was showing signs of declining into a fatal depression. I had a new girl friend, who was proving both elusive and attractive. I received a letter from one of my few relatives, which read, 'I can't think why you are being ordained. Your prayers didn't do your mother much good.'

Theological college was not a success. The students were friendly, but did not seem to believe much of what seemed important to me. The staff were similar, except for the godly but rather distant Principal. The Vice-Principal preached a sermon saying that intercessory prayer was a waste of time. I gave him a glass of sherry and interrogated him to make sure that I had heard him correctly. I had! It was time to leave. (Later I discovered that he subsequently changed his views substantially.) That winter, my father committed suicide. My world seemed to collapse. Jane, then my girl friend, was preparing to go abroad with VSO, after university, and God seemed very distant.

The Bishop of Winchester was most understanding. He encouraged me to go to St. John's Theological College, Nottingham the following September, saying that he would ordain me after one year. Without his pastoral care, I think I would have baled out. St. John's suited me much better. I enjoyed a mission in inner Manchester, and stayed on for a month to work in the parish. The mission was led by a youngish member of staff, Dr George Carey. In June 1971, I was ordained deacon, in the chapel at Winchester College, by Bishop Allison. My village rector preached. Soon afterwards, I disappeared to Papua New Guinea, to see Jane on her VSO placement.

WITH IMMEDIATE EFFECT

For the first year as a clergyman, I was just a mathematician who happened to be ordained. Then, just before my priesting, the headmaster put up a notice. JOHN WOOLMER IS APPOINTED A CHAPLAIN WITH IMMEDIATE EFFECT. My more cynical colleagues laughed— 'what effect?'

That night, we began a small mission to the school. Although not outwardly very successful, it paved the way for better things. I had started an open Christian group, and began to seek the Holy Spirit in a deeper way. At St. John's, I had been impressed and disturbed by the fervent prayer of the 'charismatics', but no-one would really explain to me what it all meant. Gradually, I started to read books about the Indonesian revival, books like *Nine o'clock in the Morning*; and to pray—especially on Saturday nights, when more sociable colleagues always seemed to be invited out to dinner. I attended a series of healing lectures, and invited Tom Smail, who was leader of the Fountain Trust, to speak at the school. After giving him supper, I asked him to pray for me. He prayed in tongues and laid hands on me. Nothing seemed to happen. He asked me about Jane (we were in a long 'cooling-off' period, stemming from the day of my priesting nine months earlier), and said that something would happen!

It did! As he prayed, she was posting me a birthday present and letter, which effectively brought us together again. A year later we were married. Around the same time, the school brought in a distinguished missioner, to give the Lenten Addresses. The talks were not a success. One housemaster bribed his boys with Mars bars, but still the average congregation was fewer than twenty. I said to the Headmaster, 'We must do better than this—can I invite Keith de Berry?'

At a rural Austrian campsite, in October 1974, I had an interesting experience. As I prayed, I noticed a nearby field. It was full of corn stooks at the bottom of the field. There was a thin line stretching up the hillside on the right of the field. God seemed to say, 'The thirty at the bottom represent those who will be converted next term—and those up the side are showing that the work will continue long afterwards.'

Keith visited the school two months later. He addressed the senior part of the school on a Wednesday afternoon, and the pupils were not pleased about having to listen to an elderly clergyman. After a few desultory moments, he told a perfectly awful joke. 'A man went into an asylum. He asked, "Why are you lot all here?" They replied, "Because we're not all there."' The school burst into laughter. The Holy Spirit took over, and Keith could do no wrong. That evening, two hundred voluntarily came to hear him speak. Seventy crowded into our small house for coffee and fuller discussion. The same happened on the next two nights. On the third night, Keith invited those who would like to respond to stay behind. About seventy did. Of these, about thirty prayed a clear prayer of commitment. Amazing things happened. I left soon afterwards, but the Christian group, under the brilliant leadership of Peter Krakenberger, grew so much that, quite often, one hundred boys attended the meetings. There were a number of significant conversions—including Richard Harvey, sometime leader of Jews for Jesus, and Mark Stibbe, now Vicar of St. Andrew's, Chorleywood. Mark felt the call of God when walking along a street in Winchester, and he compelled a reluctant and surprised Peter Krakenberger to lead him to Christ!

THE WIDER CHURCH

John Thorn, Headmaster of Winchester, gently but firmly encouraged me to get some real parish experience. He was quite right. Michael Green, then the Rector-designate of St. Aldate's, offered me a curacy. So, in April 1975, with Jane expecting our first child, we moved. I felt out of my depth. I was assigned a rather reluctant youth group, work in the 'Catacombs' (a desperately difficult, multi-racial youth club), work in the 'Flats'—part of the old Holy Trinity parish with massive social problems, and parish visiting....

I did not feel that I had much to contribute in the very talented St. Aldate's team, but I was feeling called to explore the healing ministry.

This was a difficult area in St. Aldate's at that time. Six months earlier, after my appointment, my predecessor Richard Hook had a serious car accident. The church prayed. To everyone's surprise and shock, he suddenly grew much worse and died. It did not seem tactful to raise this particular area of ministry. At that time, Michael, too, was far from convinced that the gifts of the Spirit were for today's church.

Two things happened that then propelled me, Michael and St. Aldate's into this sort of ministry. One evening, Jane and I returned from supper at which we had been asked questions about exorcism (there having been a particularly gruesome charismatic failure plastered all over the national press.) We returned reasonably early, as Jane was theoretically due to go into labour that night. A couple were waiting on the doorstep.

Reluctantly, I let them in. After about five minutes the woman said, 'My trouble is that I'm in league with the devil.'

'Why don't you renounce the devil?' I replied, rather naïvely. She suddenly let out a blood curdling scream, announcing that she renounced God. She then started prancing around our kitchen, talking and walking like an old man. I tried to telephone Michael and Rosemary to ask them to come and help. They were out to dinner with parishioners who, amazingly, were not on the phone.

'Your wife's going into labour tonight!'

'She's not. You're lying, in the name of the Lord,' I replied. (Rachel was born safely, about ten days late.)

Eventually, Michael and Rosemary arrived. The woman started 'praying' in demonic tongues—it sounded like Latin, backwards, spat out by a machine gun. Not pleasant! Michael, suspecting my charismatic gift, asked me to pray in tongues. For the first time in my life, I prayed aloud in this way. To my surprise, the woman quietened, and we began to get a grip of the situation.

This was the beginning of a very long journey, involving much ministry, including a visit by the Diocesan exorcist, who administered an anointing. The woman leapt in the air, complaining that it burnt her. She was later baptised and discipled. Many years later things seemed to have turned out well. Michael Green went off to Singapore and Australia for the summer, returning empowered in a new way by the Holy Spirit.

A few weeks after Rachel's birth, a neighbour admired her over the garden wall. Astra had deep problems—her mother had had german measles when pregnant, and Astra had been born with a terribly deformed hand. It was so painful that she wanted it amputated. Then two things happened to her, and one to me. We went on holiday in October, and I encouraged her to go and hear the Bishop of Coventry preach in St. Aldate's. We visited Jane's mother on the way to Ireland. On the Sunday she said, 'Sheila (her son's mother-in-law) is coming tomorrow. She's got a very bad back. The Lord says she's going to be healed.' I smiled politely. Sheila duly arrived, and she seemed reasonably well. I smiled to myself. I was rather sceptical of mother-in-law's gift of knowledge. The day passed and I grew more confident. Sheila, and her family, got up to leave. Quite suddenly, Sheila exclaimed that her back was giving her great pain. Her youngest daughter, aged about ten, said, 'Mummy, your back's a bore!' Sheila collapsed in tears, and wandered into the kitchen. Following her, and feeling pretty helpless, I said, 'I think my mother-in-law has a gift of healing—would you like us to pray for you?' To my horror, she said 'yes'. As Elizabeth and I prayed for her in the kitchen, we both felt a sort of current of 'spiritual electricity'. Sheila was completely healed.

The main beneficiary of the whole incident was me. Now I knew that I was called to be involved in the healing ministry. Returning from holiday, we had a pleasant surprise—Astra had been converted. She had enjoyed the Bishop's sermon, but intended to escape from the church uncommitted. But she just happened to be sitting next to Bishop Cuthbert Bardsley's wife!

Soon afterwards, she went into hospital. One day, she described my prayers as like a very powerful pain killer. When she came out of hospital, I went round to her house each evening at nine o'clock, to pray. I held her hand, and received such pain that I had to stop praying. Her hand remained deformed, but she was well enough to take a job as a taxi driver. Over the next few years we founded a healing prayer team, and Astra was involved.

Jane had suffered with serious back problems before and after Rachel's birth, so we were doubtful about having any more children. Fred Smith, a local Pentecostal leader with an 'apostolic' gift of healing, prayed for her, saying that she would never have any more serious back problems. His word proved to be right and, in due course, Susie, Tim and Katy were born without any problems.

Around three years later, Astra came to church, looking very ill. She had been diagnosed as having terminal cancer in the stomach, liver and colon—and would, perhaps live about three months. We all started to pray. Nothing much happened, except that she did not get any worse. After some five months she visited me at home. I felt that I should read the account of the healing at the Pool of Bethesda. Suddenly, I felt compelled to ask her how old she was. 'Thirty seven', she replied.

'Then you've been ill for thirty eight years!' Her illnesses stemmed back to her mother's difficult pregnancy. 'I believe you will get better' —words I have seldom felt able to say. I missed the denouement but, when a group prayed for her, she felt a great fire in her stomach, which lasted a week. Soon after, the X-rays were clear, and I had a Christmas card from her last year—twenty years later!

Michael and I were involved in many acts of deliverance. Dramatic signs accompanied some of them. Once we were having great difficulty dislodging a powerful spirit, when I felt compelled to read Zechariah 2:7. Feeling foolish, I read out 'Ho! Escape to Zion, you who dwell with the daughter of Babylon.' Michael looked triumphant. 'I know what that evil spirit is —a Babylonian mystery religion.' His intellectual knowledge, and the verse I had been given, gave us the insight we needed. Very quickly, a beautiful young lady was set free from suicide, lesbianism, and a host of other problems.

On another occasion, a young woman came to see me, announcing that she was being compelled to commit suicide. I asked her how, and was shown a huge jar of paracetamol tablets. She felt forced to say a particular word. It meant nothing to me, but I agreed to meet her that evening, with Michael. I could not find the word in my concordance, but tracked it down in the dictionary— an evil spirit mentioned in the book Tobit, who incited people to murder and suicide. That evening, when we confronted the spirit, something so powerful left the woman that it knocked Michael over.

A LOCAL CHURCH

After I had been at St. Aldate's for three years, the parish in which I was living, St. Matthew's in Grandpont, asked to rejoin St. Aldate's after about seventy years of independence. It had fallen on bad times. The congregation was mainly elderly. A retiring missionary had done valiant work for three years, and now I was asked to take over. Three key families from St. Aldate's moved into the parish to help in the work. On the day we took over, Michael and I prayed for several hours in the church, flinging wide the dusty doors, and ejecting the piles of newspapers forlornly used to boost the ailing finances of the parish. One lady walked in off the street—and joined the tiny congregation. Four exciting years followed, during which we saw a steady stream of conversions. In four years, the congregation grew to about seventy. Sixteen years later, the church is packed. The building was transformed and the whole place started to come alive.

Perhaps the most important factor was the prayer of some of the old ladies who, in the darkest days of threatened closure, prayed faithfully for the Lord to bless their church. It was a great privilege to minister in a church which served the community and also had a vision for local fellowship rather than eclectic growth. We saw healings, occasional exorcisms, some conversions, and a great growth in lay leadership. The 'every member' ministry of Ephesians 4:12 was our theological goal. Baptisms were a source of blessing. One father, understanding the gospel for the first time at his child's baptism, had a deep spiritual experience at the service. Soon afterwards, the baby was seriously ill. We prayed one evening at the house group for the little girl. It did not seem a particularly intense time of prayer. Yet there were amazing results—the baby was completely better the next day. That gave the family confidence to pray for other healing needs, and an old lady's eyesight improved dramatically.

After four years it was time to move. Two large churches contacted us. One offered me the job, and another was in the process of doing so. Meanwhile, the Bishop of Bath and Wells had asked me to apply to the Duchy of Cornwall for the living in Shepton Mallet. They replied that they had plenty of good candidates, so it was a surprise to be summoned for an interview and a greater surprise to be offered the job.

It was not a natural church for us to go to. It was of a different tradition. The previous rector had valiantly tried to modernise its approach to worship. There were three small village churches attached to the town church. We gathered our friends to pray. Eventually, a lady worker at St. Matthew's said she had a picture of a long, low, grey stone building. Jane recognised this as the rectory at Shepton Mallet. When the lady later came to our induction, she gasped and said the rectory was exactly what she had seen while we prayed. A prophetic friend gave me this 'word' over the telephone:

'Choose this day *where* you will serve. Choose the place *where, as a family*, you will all fit most naturally. I want your roots to take hold within the *whole* community and not just the body of the church. For as you are accepted and become a part—not merely as a minister but as a man, a wife, a family, within the same community, so shall the deep groundswell begin that will shake you as well as those you serve, but not that anyone shall be destroyed, but rather all shall find together that due measure of fulfilment in my name, and in my word, that is according to the need, not only of each one, but of the whole community. So choose where you most naturally fit—for you will serve for many years.'

This word pointed clearly to Shepton Mallet. The other large churches I had considered had gathered congregations, and were much less involved in the community. This was the place, with its different tradition which would shake us; this was the place that needed a reply 'today'. Despite the word that we would serve for many years, it is a surprise to be still in Shepton Mallet seventeen years later, with every prospect of staying until I retire. It is, of course, not easy to write about a ministry that is still ongoing.

THE MARKET TOWN AND VILLAGES.

When I arrived, I felt the spiritual key lay in Ephesians 4, especially verse 12: 'to prepare God's people for works of service, so that the body of Christ may be built up.' The every member ministry seemed vital if people were to grow spiritually. A rector, a curate, a reader and a parish office could not minister to 8,000 people and four churches. Each church presented a different challenge.

The tiny village of Prestleigh offered considerable light. A little group called Stable Door met to pray for healing and renewal. This group opened the way for healing services, and still provides me with venues for Alpha groups.

Cranmore had a small congregation. One night, preaching to about a dozen at their only service, I mentioned the problems of the pub which appeared to be haunted. I wondered if this cast a spiritual gloom over the parish. The reaction was unexpected. Everyone thanked me and encouraged me that this was a good starting place. We prayed from a distance. The landlord allowed us to hold services at Harvest, and provided excellent food for a regular parish dinner.

Gradually, things started to happen. One woman suffering deeply from the after effects of cancer treatment had a great spiritual experience of peace and healing when we prayed. We held a mission and some young adults were confirmed. A young mother with an ovarian cyst the size of an orange felt great release from pain when prayed for. When they came to operate, they found nothing. Apparently, her notes say, 'prayed for'. A Sunday school was started; Alpha groups have been run.

At the village of Doulting, where St. Aldhelm died in the year 709, there is a lively tradition of drama, a Sunday school, visiting team and regular healing services. When one old lady said, 'Vicar, I came to one of your healing services', I wrongly expected a negative comment. But she went on to say that she had her first real experience of God when she came forward for prayer. This enabled her to cope, with remarkable grace, humour and courage, when faced with a terminal illness soon afterwards.

What, then, of Shepton Mallet? When I arrived, I felt the key issues were prayer, worship, lay training, youth work, every member ministry, evangelism, healing and social action. Quite a list! I started a prayer group, and shocked a small but loyal group of adherents by making them pray out loud. Most have never looked back. I am convinced that prayer remains the key in the battleground. Many more people now pray alone; together, for healing; and in house groups. Early in 1999, as a result of an ordinand's dream, we planned two whole days of prayer on a Sunday. I believe these will make a significant difference to the life of the church.

Worship was very traditional. We introduced a monthly 'parish praise' service, healing services, and a midweek service led by our worship group. The latter is the service most obviously open to the gifts of the Spirit. Some of our members grew up in the Anglo-catholic tradition of the parish (retaining their views of the eucharist with integrity); we also have former house church people, evangelicals, and others who would not understand such unnecessary labels. Leaders of house groups, healing team members, readers and ordinands, and people with other ministries, have emerged from the church. One of the ordinands had come to Shepton Mallet to found a house church. Instead, he and his family joined us, and very quickly God called him to the Anglican ministry!

Evangelism has proved hard. Alpha courses have produced a trickle of converts. Others have been helped by healing, friendship, finding God in a crisis.... A number of single parents have found faith; an ex-drug taker has found peace and purpose; a reluctant parent dragged to church by his children.... There was a spiritualist 'healer' who sensed that that was not the right way, and looked for a church with a healing ministry. A number of people have been eventually helped by the faith of their husband or wife. A young man wandered into a harvest festival service and was so soundly converted that he was overcome by the Spirit when trying to explain on the telephone to his girl friend what had happened. We have tried door to door evangelism, open air services in the market place, and taking the church into some of the community centres. Despite conversions, we would like to see more fruit. It is much more difficult singing and speaking in Shepton Mallet market place on Good Friday and being largely ignored, than in a Zambian village, where they turn out in hundreds! Social action by the parish has included the setting up of a house for homeless young people. This project, largely government funded, has involved a lot of work, and occasional heartache, for the largely local management committee who oversee the house, which is run by a very professional team. Prison ministry has borne fruit with conversions.

When I had accepted the post of rector, I mentioned my interest in healing to a local newspaper, and this was reported. An unsigned letter was received, saying 'We don't want Shepton Mallet turned into Lourdes.' Over the years, we have seen some dramatic healings.There was a man with a bad knee who, after prayer, did not need an operation. There was a lady who had had a severe squint, whose oculist was amazed when he next saw her. A young woman with cancer woke with a great sense of wellbeing, and was completely better. Often in parish ministry we pray for many who do not recover, or who do not get better from long term illnesses. But, in almost every case, there is clear spiritual benefit, and often this has extended to their relatives.

I have had the joy of being involved in diocesan healing, renewal and Zambia groups. When I was chairman of the healing group, we began a series of healing services in the cathedral. One of these was particularly memorable. A man had come to see me a few days earlier, saying that he felt that he was a disturbing influence in his church and house group. I discerned that he had been involved in a lot of occult practices before his conversion, and had never renounced them. I encouraged him to come to the cathedral for prayer. When he came to me, I failed to recognise him— he had changed dramatically. He said that the evil power had left him the night before. His dramatic change also led to the conversion of his wife. While this was going on, a lady was 'resting in the Spirit', lying on the stone floor of the cathedral. She had a vision of a relative in hospital, sitting up, laughing. She knew that this relative was seriously ill, and travelled to Scotland to see him. On her first two visits he was lying in bed, obviously very ill. A few days later, she made a third visit and found him healed, sitting up in bed, laughing— just as she had 'seen' a few days earlier, when lying on the cathedral floor!

On three occasions I was involved in a SOMA (Sharing of Ministry Abroad) team visit to Zambia, and saw many miracles. Once, I saw an archdeacon so filled with the Spirit that I am ashamed to say that I thought he was drunk. (cf Acts 2:13); one man who was totally deaf in one ear was healed so completely that he joined the choir; a churchwarden who gave out a notice: 'Tomorrow, brethren, we will see signs and wonders.'

The most astonishing supernatural experience I have seen took place in 1992 at Muto Wan Koko ('the village of the severed chicken's head'). I preached to some five hundred people in the open air. It was a beautiful day. There was dancing by the Mothers' Union. Blue Charaxes butterflies danced around the top of the mango trees. Everyone listened intently. Suddenly, I felt that I must challenge them to really renounce witchcraft and throw away their charms given by the medicine men. I think this was partly inspiration, and partly because I had had such a difficult period of ministry after the first session, with almost everyone manifesting evil spirits as soon as they had received prayer for their healing.

I was aware of hollow laughter and asked my interpreter (the Spirit-filled archdeacon, who now had an amazing ministry of healing and deliverance) what was going on. He replied, 'They have so little and now you are asking them to give things to us!' For almost the only time in my life, I felt the righteous anger of God and spoke perhaps too fiercely. Afterwards, I felt quite worn out and ashamed. What right had I, a mere visitor, who did not know their culture, to speak like that?

The next day, a smaller crowd, perhaps three hundred, gathered in the church. As we were about to begin, a lady asked to speak. This was most unusual. She was not even a member of the Mothers' Union! Her face shone with a supernatural light. Her story (told in Bemba, then translated for me) was that she had walked to the church in the half-light of the early morning. She saw a figure dressed in white following her. She thought this was odd. No Zambians wear white clothes. She went around one side of the church; the figure went the other way. She went to meet him—and found no-one! She was quite convinced it was an angel; so was everyone else. We had a remarkable morning of evangelism and healing and, after lunch, left a happy crowd behind. The Blue Charaxes butterflies continued to dance in the trees. Some years later, I again met Father James, the Vicar of Muto. He cycled fifty miles to join our fourth SOMA team, and testified to the power of the Spirit and the spiritual wellbeing of the woman who saw the angel.

I am so grateful to God for the support of Jane and all my four children, loyal, hardworking and praying congregations, and supportive church leaders. It has been a privilege to write, to speak elsewhere in England and abroad, and above all to pray with those in real need. Over the years, by the grace of God, I have been able to go on learning, including things from other traditions of the church. During a wonderful month as part of a sabbatical at the Franciscan Friary at Hilfield, I started writing *Thinking Clearly about Prayer*. Quiet, contemplative prayer with twenty others was a helpful way of beginning the day— and inspirational for writing. I have seen God answer many prayers and, when the answer has been 'no', I have usually seen why. Like others, I wonder why the 'signs of the Kingdom' seem so much more abundant in Africa than in England. I puzzle over the difficulties of evangelism, and people's contentment with a nominal faith, declared enthusiastically at baptisms and weddings.

I did not want to be a clergyman. I was happy teaching mathematics at Winchester College. But I have to admit that God knew best, and I am grateful for His call, and for His Holy Spirit, who changed a shy and inward-looking bachelor—enabling me to enjoy relating to people in a myriad of different cultures and situations.

Note: Some material in this chapter has also appeared in THINKING CLEARLY ABOUT HEALING AND DELIVERANCE, Monarch £7.99.

'Recovering His Reputation'

STUART BELL

Rector of Aberystwyth

'Why on earth do you want to go there?' I asked my friend when he told me that he had chosen Aberystwyth as his University. I could not think of anywhere more remote from Torquay. My impression of it was that it was on the road to nowhere, at the end of the railway line and not particularly attractive. We had visited Aberystwyth when I was nine, on a family holiday, and my only recollection was of sitting on a stony beach, getting tar on my trousers and being in trouble for it—so I was not going to recommend that anyone should actually choose to go there. Had I known then that it was sometimes called 'the town for the unambitious man' I would have tried still harder to change his mind.

He didn't listen to me, and ended up there as a student, and I didn't listen to me either, because twenty five years later I came here as the Rector of the parish. I wonder what God thought when He heard me running the place down. Perhaps this was just another of those occasions when He had a good laugh.

In fact, Aberystwyth has turned out to be a delightful place to live. The Cambrian mountains meet Cardigan Bay with glorious views of the Lleyn peninsula out to sea and lovely countryside inland which stretches for miles. The town is much less run down than it was and with large injections of money in recent years it has developed more and more as a centre of commercial and administrative importance. M&S, that great statement of advancing civilisation, has not yet reached us, but McDonald's has, so we have almost arrived.

The combination of ministry to the local town population, the students and academic staff of the University, the hospital, the National Library of Wales, as well as the large numbers of tourists who visit us in the summer, ensures that we are kept busy all the year round. As a result, we never face the tragedy of some churches where the same people, and only the same people, will turn up Sunday after Sunday. Sometimes it has been a Japanese bishop in the congregation, or two Poles who happened to be visiting the area, or the local woman who phoned today saying 'I must talk to you because I need to come back to God'; or those who are coming and hardly know why or how they are there. In this mixed 'town and gown', cosmopolitan and yet definitely Welsh seaside resort, God is at work.

The Torquay of my boyhood was good preparation for living and working in another holiday resort. The ebb and flow of the visitors, the feeling that 'this is not my home' during the season, the relief when the tourists go away again, the sense that we need them for our own financial survival, the 'tack' they bring with them, the seasonal businesses and seasonal employment. It all has such a familiar feel to it. Yet without my conversion to Christ this link between seaside resorts would have been largely irrelevant to me.

At the age of twelve, my brother wanted to take me to Hele Road Baptist Church in Torquay, where he was attending regularly, and I had no intention of joining him. We were a 'Poppy Day only' family at that time. As my father had died just after the war, as a result of his service in Burma, it was family custom to go to church on Remembrance Sunday, but only then. We never went at Christmas nor Easter, nor any other time. The solemnity of the occasion was always disturbed by giggles from the Bell pew as we tried our very best to follow the Book of Common Prayer but, because no-one told us where we were in the book, we were usually completely lost. Just when we thought we had found the right place, the vicar disappeared somewhere else in the book and we were lost again—usually trying to look over the shoulders of the people in front, to see if they had any more idea than we had.

On this particular morning, my brother was especially persuasive and even got my mother to join in getting me to go to church with him. I gave them a very difficult time, but ultimately and very unwillingly agreed to go to the Baptist Church. That day the pastor, the Rev. David Abernethie, was preaching about the cross. I heard for the very first time that Jesus had died for me. I must have known about Calvary before then, but I never knew that I was personally involved. It made such an impression on me that I went back again that evening voluntarily, and even stayed to the youth meeting which was held afterwards.

That was the beginning of my coming to Christ. The barb on the hook of the Christian faith had penetrated my soul and I was caught for life. Calvary has always held me. When, some years later, I did one of the *CWR* counselling courses and was asked the standard question, 'Write down where your security, significance and self-worth lie', I put 'the cross of Calvary' in the answer box to each question and did so not because I thought that that ought to be the correct answer but because it is true for me. From that day to this, the cross has burned in my soul as the expression of God's love and care for me. It has become very personal, and something from which I cannot and do not want to escape.

Perhaps it was that day that I became a Christian, or maybe it was after the visit of John Wesley White, who was an associate evangelist with the Billy Graham Evangelistic Association. He preached very effectively one Sunday evening in Hele Road Baptist Church, and I was totally caught up in what he had been saying. He closed his sermon with an appeal that if anyone wanted to respond to Christ then they should pray a prayer quietly after him, and then if they had prayed that prayer they should look up at him. I didn't know anything about 'rolling appeals' at that time, but next he invited those who had looked at him to come to the front during the last hymn and 'especially that young man sitting at the back'! I have seen and heard other evangelists using the same technique occasionally since then, and have always thought that they are being insensitive.

I was taken to the vestry, and there a Moorlands Bible College Student with very bad breath took me through a commitment to Christ. What has remained in my mind ever since that day is Romans 10:9–10, which he underlined in a copy of the New Testament he gave me. 'If you confess with your mouth 'Jesus is Lord' and believe in your heart that God raised him from the dead, you will be saved. For it is with your heart that you believe and are justified, and it is with your mouth that you confess and are saved.'

After that, I responded to Christ in the way that a teenager responds to everything, with enthusiasm one minute and with total indifference the next. As a result, I was sometimes more on fire than Billy Graham and put Christian tracts into the desks of my friends, and at other times I joined in the dirty stories of a Boys' Grammar School with as much abandon as anyone.

'The Hound of Heaven' is a most glorious description of the Holy Spirit for, in the early part of the term, in the Upper Sixth, God began to close in on me. At this stage, my commitment to Him was seriously lacking as all the other temptations and ambitions of adolescence were pressing in on me, but still God was doing His secret work in me. Increasingly, despite the fact that I was determinedly not following the Lord, I became more and more aware that He was calling me to the full time ministry. No-one else was involved in this, although occasional comments were made to me as I was still attending church at least once a Sunday, and that was rare for teenagers even then.

By this time I had become an Anglican, because being baptised by immersion in the Baptist Church required a public testimony to conversion, and I was terrified by such a thought. It was much easier to be confirmed with the Anglicans 'no questions asked' and become a good and godly member of the church choir— or so everyone thought.

I have met one other person during my ministry who felt called to ordination before he had given his life fully to Christ, and he actually became a committed Christian at a CPAS *You and the Ministry* conference! That is a bit back to front, but it does seem that God has very few rules concerning the way that He deals with us.

One of the local churches at Torre in Torquay was always open during the day. So every afternoon, when school was over, there I was—a seventeen year old sixth former with God breathing down my neck. I was on my knees and asking the Lord to accept me. That was the prayer I offered from Monday to Friday, but by the Friday evening I knew that my prayer had been answered and that the contract was sealed. I was the Lord's and the Lord was mine. How did I know? I just knew that I knew. 'His Spirit was witnessing with my spirit that I was a child of God' [Rom 8:16], but I did not then know that that was the way to explain it. But it was not just that I knew, so did others in school. Quickly, some of my friends who were Christians were asking what had happened to me. I was able to tell them that their prayers for me had been answered.

The changes which took place in my personal life were dramatic where I was concerned, although perhaps others would not have been so aware of them. There was a new desire to live for Christ, and a brand new attitude to life. Previously, I had been longing to get away to college so that I could sow my wild oats, but now my ambitions and even my dreams had changed.

One person whom I was particularly glad to tell was Jim Stokes, my Crusader leader. Despite all the ups and downs of my teenage faith, Jim had been a faithful and godly example to me and had taught me almost as much about the Bible as my theology degree at University was going to teach me. Undoubtedly, he had given me a good overview of the Scriptures and had taught me that they could be trusted. He did not just teach us lads that they were true but he lived it in his own life. I owe him a great debt of gratitude and was able to tell him so on a number of occasions. The last time was when being lifted into a wheelchair, crippled and twisted by Parkinson's Disease and almost incomprehensible in his speech. I said to him, 'Jim, you have been so faithful to the Lord.' He replied, 'He has been so faithful to me.' That was the kind of quality godliness I had had lived in front of my eyes.

So, convinced of this call from God that I should be ordained, it seemed natural to me to study theology at university. I moved twenty miles up the road to Exeter University, which seemed like the other end of the world to a car-less family.

My first concern was that I would stand as a Christian in an environment which I knew was likely to be hostile. For several weeks before the beginning of the first term, I asked the Lord for a Christian in my digs, so that I would have someone there to encourage me and keep me on track. It was delightful and amazing to find that I was sharing a room with a mature Christian graduate from Cambridge, who was doing a teaching diploma at St. Luke's. His company, solidity and well-thought out faith helped me enormously as did his morning prayer which he uttered aloud, 'Lord, let my waking thought be of thee.'

Throughout the university Christian Unions of the mid 1960s, there was extensive debate about the charismatic renewal, and Exeter was no exception. The Fountain Trust was being formed then, and the whole matter of being 'baptised in the Spirit' was being hotly and constantly discussed within the CU and by the IVF travelling secretaries. Books were being read, sermons preached, talks given and many of our fellow students were entering into deeper experiences of God than the majority of us had ever been led to believe was possible.

Somehow or another I, like most of my fellow Christians at that time, had got the idea that we had a great experience of the Lord at conversion, but that that was virtually all there was to be had. It was a matter of holding on grimly until we got to glory. Our experience of worship was flat and dull, our expectation of God was severely limited, and our experience of the presence and activity of the Spirit was rare. Suddenly, on all sides, there were other Christians who were saying that there was much much more than that. Fairly regularly, members of the CU were catching fire spiritually and were entering into a deeper experience of the Lord. It was obvious from their prayers in the prayer meeting. The 'what has happened to you?' question was often being asked amongst the Christians.

This intense spiritual environment set me looking for a similar touch from the Lord. After reading *They Speak with other Tongues* by Sherrill, I knelt in my room and asked the Lord to fill me with His Spirit. The book had suggested that the 'normal Pentecostal' method of being filled by the Spirit in the United States was that people were encouraged to raise their hands in the air and to begin to praise the Lord. I wrestled all alone in my room, thinking that I was an idiot, that God didn't respond to this kind of mechanical nonsense, that He was not a slot machine— and all of the other good Christian arguments for not doing anything of the kind.

It then occurred to me that no-one else was there, and that no-one else would know what I had been doing in the privacy of my room unless of course I were to tell them. So, finally, after wrestling over the issue for some time, I raised my arms to the Lord and spoke out 'Hallelujah'. What followed was the most awful feeling of foolishness, which lasted for just a split second; then, quite suddenly and unexpectedly, the Lord filled me as I had never ever been filled before. Living worship flowed from my lips, but more especially from my heart. I touched heaven that evening, and heaven touched me.

What followed was a faith which was more on fire than ever and more effective than ever. I wanted still more and began to pray daily at length. Then one evening, as I was out for a run, I was thinking about the Lord, praying and enjoying His presence as I ran down the pedestrian way to St. David's station in Exeter. It seemed as though the Lord was right there. The words came to my lips, 'Jesus is coming' and I spoke them out. As I did so, tongues began to flow freely. That was the beginning of my personal experience of the charismatic gifts, which has continued unabated for over thirty years.

On arrival at university, one of the decisions I had taken before the Lord was that I was willing to be celibate for Him, if that was what He wanted. I do not recall how I had come to that conclusion, as it had not been raised as an issue in any of the churches or meetings that I had attended, but I was aware that the choice of marriage partner can make or break a person's spiritual life and ministry, and also that matters of the heart are hugely complicated. I had not heard Canon Keith de Berry's advice at that time to 'only marry someone who is more godly than you'. That is a piece of impossible advice because either one or the other partner in the marriage would be disobeying the principle, but it certainly makes the right point.

However, for all my sincerity and determination to be celibate, within the first week I was to meet the woman who, four years later, was to become my wife. Pru was already a student in Exeter, training as an occupational therapist at St. Loyes College, and had been converted some months earlier through a talk given by the very same Keith de Berry at a Lee Abbey Students Houseparty. I sometimes wonder whether my promised commitment to celibacy was another occasion when I made God laugh. At the time I felt rather like Abraham who had taken Isaac as far as the mountain of sacrifice and actually had the knife in his hand before the Lord said, 'Now I know that you love me'. On this issue the Lord was able to say, 'I know that you love me', because I would have remained celibate if He had called me to it. As the years have gone past, I wonder how on earth I would have survived though, and perhaps the Lord wondered that at the time too, which is why He never put me through it!

One other matter which was resolved whilst I was at University was where I should serve the Lord. The answer had already been given to Him by me—anywhere. When we had sung and prayed 'all on the altar we lay' I had meant every word of it. Wherever the Lord called me to go, to whichever continent, whatever climate, whatever circumstances, whatever language, whatever culture barriers, I would go. He knew I was serious, and so did I. In that, there has been no change.

During my time as a student, I had been processed as a potential ordinand, attended the selection conference, and had been conditionally accepted. It was clear to me and to everyone else that I was a very young man with no experience of life, and it would have been disastrous for me to proceed from school to university to theological college to ordination, without having had the opportunity to find out what real life was like. Coventry was one of the growth towns of Britain at that time, and the Director of Ordinands in Exeter suggested that I should go there and find a job.

Within a few weeks I was driving a bread delivery van around Binley in Coventry and my education was beginning. The supervisor responsible for me had the nickname of Effy, for obvious reasons, and he used swear words that I had never ever heard before. Strangely enough, there was another trainee ordinand working for Suttons Bakery at the time and he also was doing a retail round. The poor lad could not do his sums, and he constantly came back short at the end of the week and had to make the money up from his own pocket. He didn't last long. For me, though, somehow or another I always seemed to have money left over when cashing up, and would use the extra money to pay off some of my customers' bad debts. The other men found that surprising and would comment, 'You're not using your fiddle to pay off the debts are you?' 'Fiddle' was taken for granted as part of the perks of the job. Another education.

One of the customers on the breadround was Peter Larkin, who at that time had finished as a curate in Rugby and was now working full time on Bishop Cuthbert Bardsley's *Call to Mission*. This was intended to be a diocesan evangelistic initiative, of which Bishop Cuthbert himself was the inspiration. He was also to be the main missioner. Peter had a vacancy in his expanding office and took me on as an administrative assistant. The work was routine, but the opportunity to be at the hub of an evangelistic programme of such a scale was thrilling. For me, the highlight was the invitation to make a personal faith statement at one of the main mission meetings, in front of a packed cathedral congregation and hundreds of other people in overflow meetings in buildings close by.

The week after the end of the mission, Pru and I left Coventry for Exeter, where we were going to marry. I had a very generous cheque from Bishop Cuthbert in my pocket as a wedding present, and Peter Larkin was going to perform the ceremony for us in what had been our student church of St. Leonard's. The very same day, Jacqueline Kennedy the widow of JFK married Aristotle Onassis. I do not suppose that they ever knew that there was another important wedding taking place that day.

From being an administrative assistant I moved to the draw-twisting department of Courtaulds on the Foleshill Road. At that stage, they were working on the development of carbon fibres, which were considered to be at the cutting edge of scientific development. My work colleagues turned out to be a real hotchpotch of nationalities. Onc, a Scot, was a serious minded Christian and he was fascinated to find me reading a copy of the life story of Andrew Bonar — one of his own countrymen. There was a Ukrainian, who taught me about the 'Safety and New Ideas' box, which allowed employees to make suggestions to the management about the better running of the department. Subsequently, I was on regular bonuses for ideas and new proposals. Then there was the Asian who, when I got a copy of the Bible in Gujarati for him, admitted that he could not read it and would have preferred one in English. All that effort to get him the Bible, but it was good intentions with little wisdom and that was what I was there to gain. How do you get experience? By making mistakes. How do you avoid making mistakes? By getting experience.

During our time in Coventry, like most Midlanders, we made occasional forays into Wales for day trips. We visited unpronounceable villages and mountains and reservoirs, appreciating the grandeur and beauty of what we saw. But something happened during the summer of 1969, which made us look at Wales in quite a different way. Pru and I were on a hitch-hiking tour of North Wales. The B&B where we spent the night in Bala was being run by the wife of one of the local policemen. He was a good Presbyterian and we began to talk about the great spiritual heritage of Wales, the powerful preachers of the past, the godliness of whole communities, and the impact of revivals which followed one another in quick succession. What surprised and disappointed me was to hear from him that the sound of revival remained in the hymns and the singing, but that it had been lost from the heart of the Welsh people.

It was a tragic story and, when we attended an English service the next morning in a local Nonconformist church, it was easy to see what our policeman friend was talking about. The atmosphere was deadly, so was the singing, and so too the sermon. How would anyone be drawn to Christ through that kind of church?

As we left Bala to travel further north, a romantic notion of coming to Wales 'in order to do something about the situation' had already settled in my soul. Remarkably, the more we prayed about it the more the desire grew. It was one of those ideas which simply would not go away. It continued to grow in our thinking and praying and, as always when God is trying to get through to us, 'everything was coming up Welsh'! It seemed to come into so many conversations and allusions in books. Suddenly, Wales seemed to be headline news, or at least it was to us.

The following year, when I began training at Tyndale Hall Theological College in Bristol, the most natural thing was to join the local Welsh society and begin the process of learning Welsh. It was clear right from the outset that the Welsh language is the key to the soul of the nation. If the whole of the southern seaboard of Wales was won to Christ and the cities of Cardiff, Newport and Swansea were Christian to the last man and woman, we would not have won Wales back to Christ. The soul of the nation is in the Welsh speaking population and their soul needs to be addressed in their own language. One woman once said to me, 'If you tell me in English I'll understand it, but if you tell me in Welsh I'll understand it and take it in'. Language study began in earnest.

Whilst at college it was the normal procedure for students to have some first hand experience of parish life during the long summer vacation, and the only other Tyndale man who was in Wales was Bill Lewis, then Vicar of Letterston in Pembrokeshire. We spent three weeks with him and his family and, within a fortnight, there was no doubt remaining that this was the way forward for us. Bill was pastoring a small rural church which embraced the entire community. The family services were thronged with people, and his ministry was obviously making a difference. Because of the nature of village life, he was in touch with all the families in the area, there were conversions, spiritual growth, and a sense that the church was on the move.

The next step was to see the Director of Ordinands for the St. David's diocese, and this was arranged at very short notice. He asked some tough questions like, 'What do think you've got to offer the Church in Wales?' But that interview was followed within days by another one with the Diocesan Training Committee. Again, I was faced by some hostility, not least by one member of the committee who asked me, 'Why do you think that there are so few people from your Theological College serving in Wales?' I was too naïve to know the answer at that time. It certainly would have been inappropriate to answer, 'Because you don't want Evangelicals in the Church in Wales'. Mercifully, the interview concluded with Bishop John Richards assuring me that I had been accepted into the diocese, 'And,' he whispered in my ear, 'we need more Evangelicals in the St. David's diocese'. That was a good thing to hear because he was just about to get another one!

Being accepted by the Bishop and the Training committee was one thing, but finding a parish willing to take a young Englishman with a call to work in the Church in Wales was quite another matter. I began to make enquiries through Bill Lewis, but each door we tried seemed to be solidly closed. One parish that we had visited during the previous summer was Aberaeron, on the west coast of Wales. On one particularly attractive day, when the sun was shining, the yachts were riding high on their moorings in the harbour, and the colourwashed houses were looking especially stunning, we stood looking over the town and said to one another, 'Wouldn't it be lovely to be vicar here?'

We actually met the vicar of Aberaeron, Bertie Lewis, during that visit, but he made it clear that it would be necessary for him to have a bilingual curate, as it was about 80% Welsh speaking My language studies were still in their infancy at that time. The months passed. Bishop John Richards retired and there was an interregnum in the diocese. There was no-one to make any plans for the soon-to-be-ordained curates and no place for us to go. With Easter 1971 fast approaching, all the other students leaving Tyndale Hall had found parishes to begin their ministry. Then, quite unexpectedly, a letter arrived from Bertie Lewis, saying that he had reconsidered his own position. He felt that it might be possible to offer me a curacy after all. Because of my college commitments and his parish duties, there was no chance of a visit to Aberaeron to see him until Easter Monday, and that was the day that he offered me the opportunity to become his curate. I accepted, and our lives became intertwined in quite a remarkable way. In April it was agreed. In May, the new bishop was consecrated. In June, we moved to Aberaeron, I was ordained and parish ministry began.

The most remarkable confirmation that we were in the right place doing the right thing came at my ordination. The first hymn was under way and the procession into St. David's cathedral had begun. The ordinands, with me amongst them, were following the choir down the side aisle, with the clergy, canons and bishop behind us, when I heard a voice speaking from just behind my shoulder which said, 'This is the way, walk in it'. It was so clear that I turned to look to see who was speaking to me, and there were only other members of the procession getting into another verse of *Onward Christian Soldiers*.

To say that I was green and ignorant is an understatement. I knew nothing. The one gift I had was enthusiasm, but I was willing to learn, and the good judgement, sound common sense and practical godliness which I saw in Bertie Lewis have been a kind of benchmark for my own ministry ever since. I had heard others speak about the need for a good training in your first parish, but I had been so desperate to get into the Church in Wales that that had been low down on my list of priorities. Mercifully, the Lord knew, and saw to it that I was trained by one of the best parish clergymen in Wales.

Language study continued. By the time that I arrived in Aberaeron, I was able to read the liturgy in Welsh, even if I couldn't understand it! That sounds familiar somehow! How many people have difficulty with the liturgy, even when it is in their own mother tongue? During that time, the Wlpan course was being established as a method of language learning, which imitated the system used by the Israelis for teaching Hebrew to immigrants. It involves a total immersion in the language, so I was travelling thirty miles a night, five nights a week, for a two-hour language lesson in Aberystwyth – that town for the unambitious man.

The course was coming to an end and, one morning, after opening the post, I stood near the fireplace of our little curate's house and read out to Pru a letter from the bishop, offering me the parish of Llangeler. 'Pull the other one!' was Pru's immediate response, because we had spent many of our days off over the previous months driving around the countryside, looking at rural churches and measuring ourselves against the needs of the local parishes. Talking about moving was part of our regular conversation. I just longed to get out and do it 'alone'.

Once I had convinced Pru that the letter was genuine, we had to find out where Llangeler was. Predictably, it was one church we had not looked at, most particularly because it was in a strongly Welsh speaking area. It is in the heart of the countryside, in the very beautiful Teifi Valley, twenty miles inland from Cardigan, and is described as 'the Garden of Carmarthenshire'. The 'advantage' of the parish was that they had never known a vicar who would speak to them in English. It was clearly going to be a risk for everyone. A risk for the parish, a risk for us, and a risk for the Bishop, but he did give us an assurance that if it did not work out, then after a couple of years he would move us on again.

This really was going to be a challenge, for an English 'townie' to cross the language and culture barriers, and identify with an ancient and still very vibrant culture in a rural Welsh community. Jack Deere has said that, 'the clearer the revelation, the harder the task.' Often, it was only the certainty of the call of God which kept us going at all.

Difficult or not, we faced the challenge with determination. At my induction, after we had locked and unlocked the main door as part of the ceremony, we then came to ringing the bell. I asked the church warden for help, because I have always had trouble getting church bells to ring properly. He knew as well as I did that all the clergy were listening, to hear how many times the bell tolled. The tradition is one year for every pull of the bell rope. As we held onto the bell rope together, he whispered to me, 'How many?' I replied, 'thirty six!' He didn't seem to appreciate my sense of humour at that moment, so we settled for half a dozen. But the offer of thirty six was more than a leg-pull. I wanted him to know that I was serious about the commitment of my life to the Welsh nation and the cause of the Gospel in Wales.

This call to Wales has dominated our ministry for three decades. I have very rarely accepted invitations to minister outside the province, and have turned down a number of very attractive job offers in England, even quite recently. There has been no need to pray about them, as this is the place that the Lord has called us to. The offer of anything else is simply a distraction. Just as Nehemiah had been called by the Lord to rebuild the walls of Jerusalem and refused to allow anything else to come in the way, so we feel that any work outside of Wales is a distraction and a drain on the energies which we are to invest here.

It is strange that the call should be so clear, as I have no blood ties with Wales whatsoever, but interestingly Pru has a strong Welsh pedigree, which has become more and more important to us as the years have gone by. Her great-grandmother Elisabeth Williams, from Llysyfran in Pembrokeshire, married Herbert Dixon, a doctor, and the two of them went to China to be medical missionaries. They were both martyred during the Boxer rebellion in 1900, and there is a Welsh language memorial tablet to Elisabeth in Tabernacl Chapel in St. David's. In addition, Pru still has distant cousins living in that area.

I owe the parish of Llangeler a great debt of gratitude, for they were so patient with me. They remained loyal, despite so many of my insensitivities. That is not to say that it was all plain sailing. It was not. I would have to go home at 4 p.m. on many an occasion, and finish my afternoon visiting early, because I had a pounding headache as several hours of conversation in a new language was such a strain. On a Sunday afternoon, at the end of my third service of the day, I would drive home exhausted, unable to get the car out of third gear and go more than fifteen miles per hour. On one occasion, standing in the hallway of the Vicarage, I told the Lord, 'I don't mind dying for you; it's the pain I can't stand.'

Work on improving my Welsh continued daily. The thing that surprised me most of all was that people spoke Welsh on the phone. I still cannot understand quite why I was so surprised at that. It did make things more difficult because, like most language students, I was depending on lip reading to a certain extent. One of the other things to do was to cross from the language of books and the classroom to the language as spoken, and particularly as spoken in the Teifi Valley. Ultimately, the imprint of the education they gave me has had an indelible effect on me. I still speak Teifi Valley Welsh.

This learning of a new language, and identifying with a new culture, has received many comments over the years, perhaps mostly because it has all taken place within the British Isles. Ignorance of Welshness in England is deplorable, but I well remember picking up Welsh language broadcasts on my transistor whilst in my teens, and thinking that it was a language which was just spoken by a few obscure academics who wanted to keep it going. Now I have discovered that I stand in a long line of Christians, beginning with the apostle Paul, who recognised that identifying culturally with the area where you are going with the Gospel is one of the imperatives of the Christian message. He was willing to be a Jew amongst the Jews and a Gentile amongst the Gentiles, in order that, 'by all means he might save some'. All that he was doing was climbing into the cultural mind-set of the people he was working with, in order to present Christ effectively to them. There have been others, throughout the history of the church, who have done similar things. Not least, Hudson Taylor and the Cambridge Seven, who grew pigtails and wore Chinese clothes for their work with the China Inland Mission. Such cultural and linguistic identification is happening throughout the world for the sake of Christ, but it is always a surprise that it is necessary in Britain too.

Within weeks of being in Llangeler, I had made some terrible mistakes, but over six years we had done some things that many would have said were impossible. The congregations in the main church had trebled, we had established house groups for all the churches, developed a youth work and had seen many people grow in their faith. Some came to faith for the very first time. All the while I was there, I longed to have the wisdom of Bertie Lewis, and would constantly ask myself the question, 'If he was faced with this problem, what would he do?' Often I would ring him to find out.

Can we? Can't we? These were questions we began to ask ourselves after just two years. Can we stay on? Can't we move on? The language study was tough. The progress we were making was slow, as is always true in rural communities. The cultural bridges seemed to be too difficult to erect from our side. It was at that time that I was preaching on Elijah and using F.B. Meyer's book about him for preparation and study. He has a chapter devoted to the hidden ministry of Elijah at the brook Cherith, and we felt that in many ways those years were years of hidden ministry, which prepared us for what was to come. The thought was of little comfort, because the pain of the ministry was still very great at times. But there was nonetheless a reality about that particular spiritual truth which could not simply be ignored.

As our sixth year in Llangeler was drawing to a close, we were once again in the process of measuring ourselves against this parish and that parish, and looking up in the Diocesan Year Book the names of all the clergy whose retirement would create vacancies. Of all the places we looked at and thought about, there was one which never ever entered our minds. Soon after we had left the parish of Aberaeron, Bertie Lewis also moved, to be vicar of Lampeter. He was followed by a new incumbent who, as far as we knew, was settled and would not want to move for a good few years. Quite unexpectedly, we started to hear rumours that he was unsettled and looking for a move; that he had been appointed to another parish, and then, no longer a rumour, that he was actually leaving. Some of the parish representatives in Aberaeron were keen that we should apply, returning to the town as vicar.

The idea was so totally unexpected that it had to have a touch of the hand of God about it. Never had my mind or day-dreaming strayed back to the parish where I had done my curacy, but now that the idea had been raised it was a very attractive proposition. We had been told at theological college that, 'the Lord is likely to give you one really pleasant parish', but if we were to return then this meant a second bite of a lovely cherry for us. As it turned out, I was the first horse in a one horse race, for no-one else applied. So, in 1980, we returned to Aberaeron, to become vicar of the parish where those ten years before we had stood on the quayside and said, 'Wouldn't it be lovely to be vicar here?' Was God laughing again or just being very very good to us? Or perhaps both.

The first hurdle to overcome was to be the vicar and not the curate but in fact there was hardly any problem at all over that. Six years had passed. We had moved on, and so had the parish. We had the pleasure of consolidating the work that had been done previously and seeing further developments in the spiritual life of the parish. A house group programme was established, several prayer groups, regular evenings

51

of prayer and fasting for the life of the church, and a leadership team drawn together of clergy and lay leaders. There were conversions, and more and more the life of the church made an impact on the town.

These were real family years for us. Our children—Julia, born nine years earlier; Isaac (five); and Rhiannon (two), enjoyed the large Vicarage, the extensive grounds, and the excellent education on offer in the town. It was a superb environment for them, in which to grow up. God was being good and generous to the whole family.

It is quite strange to find that you know when your time somewhere is at an end. After eight years of this second period of time in Aberaeron, I knew that it was time to be on the move. There seems to come a time in a parish when people have finally got you in their pocket. I felt that I had arrived at a point when people could say 'no' to me—a very dangerous time for a clergyman. I had given all that I had to, and had run out of ideas and vision for the parish. Another person with different gifts was needed, to come and try to persuade them to move forward. Once again, we began the process of looking around. As before, there was one decisive condition laid down for the new parish, and that was that it had to be bilingual. Learning Welsh had been such a costly task that it was, and is, inconceivable that we would ever work outside a bilingual setting. Cardigan had a vicar who was just about to retire; the church held Welsh services, and the town was double the size of Aberaeron and would expand my ministry. I needed advice, so I went to call on Bertie Lewis.

By this time, he had moved from Lampeter to Aberystwyth and had done a tremendous work in the parish. When he arrived in the town the main church of St. Michael's had about seventy in the congregation in the morning and twenty five in the evening. Within a few years, the morning congregation had trebled and the evening had increased almost eight fold. He had had a charismatic experience of his own, which had brought his ministry into a new dimension, and this coincided with something of a revival amongst the young people of the area as well as his own congregation. The young people were accused of forming a 'God squad' in Penglais School, and there was a lot of fuss in the local paper, but many of them found in St. Michael's a church where they were sympathetically and enthusiastically pastored. Some of the more traditional members found the changes difficult to handle, and left for other churches in the area. But, in spite of criticism, Bertie Lewis exercised a courageous and divinely blessed ministry, which saw people in tears as they came into the building and others powerfully converted.

When I called at Aberystwyth Rectory to ask Bertie what he thought about me applying for Cardigan, he surprised me totally when he told me that he was planning to move, because by this time he had been Archdeacon as well as Rector for the past two years. He felt that he was not doing justice to either post. His comment was, 'You must follow me here'. So, once again we were faced by the completely unexpected. All of the questioning, 'Is this the place? Is that the place?' was wasted because the Lord was calling us in a direction that we could never have foreseen. We now try to live in the predictability of the unpredictable, for we have seen it happen so often in our own experience. The statement that 'if you want to make God laugh then tell him your plans' has got a particular significance for us.

My name had to be submitted to the Diocesan Patronage Board, and once again I turned out to be the first horse in a one-horse race. In April 1988 I was inducted as Rector. I felt like Rehoboam inheriting the kingdom from Solomon. As the new man, taking over the helm, I knew that no congregation can ever stand still: the parish could so easily go either into further growth, or backwards into stagnation. Trying to maintain the status quo is a death knell for any church. The need for wisdom was great.

It has been well said that rarely do churches committed to evangelism suffer division. When the attention and focus of the congregation is on winning to Christ those who are unchurched, the consequence is that they do not have time or energy for feuds and disagreements amongst themselves. This was not the reason for adopting the single word 'growth' as the watch-word of the congregation, but the side-effect of such an emphasis has been to hold the whole church together.

In 1990, St. Michael's Church held its centenary celebrations and one objective was that we would seek to win one hundred people to Christ during the year—one for every year of the existence of the building. We did not get anywhere near that target but, as a stated desire, it was a glorious emphasis, and every activity was intended to have an evangelistic purpose. It was also the beginning of the decade of evangelism and, in order to take hold of that vision, the four churches of the benefice covenanted together to do at least one act of evangelism together each year during the decade. We would either do it together in concert, or we would do something at the same time, in and through our individual churches. This agreement has been kept to, and has grown from small guest events at the beginning of the decade to a town-wide interdenominational Holy Week Mission in 1999, with a team of forty missioners, under the leadership of Canon Michael Green.

Our repeated prayer is for 'wall-to-wall' congregations and, under God, we have seen the church continue to grow. In the last ten years, St. Michael's has doubled in size again. Now, every Sunday morning the building is full almost to capacity, with townspeople, tourists and students. We have a few low Sundays when the students go, before the main flood of tourists arrive, but that is an important family time when the permanent congregation draws breath for the next period of ministry.

Prayer has been the foundation stone of all the progress we have seen. For over five years, we had a 6 a.m. prayer meeting three times a week, when we would pray for the Lord's blessing and for revival in the church. Regrettably, this became unsustainable because of the commitment required, but there were some heavenly times together. We now meet at a more civilised time of 7.15 a.m. on a Wednesday and 7.30 p.m. on a Friday, together with other more ad hoc groups. Although, as in every church, the number of those who feel a call to the intercessory ministry is not large, there is nonetheless a solid base of those who are committed to pray—and there is no area of church life which is not prayed for.

We are absolutely convinced that the Lord has not called us to preside over a declining church heading for extinction in Wales. The statistics of church closures, falling membership rolls and retirement of clergy give a picture of a God in retreat. We are determined that that trend will be reversed.

It has been well said that, 'Retreat as a tactic is sometimes necessary: retreat as a settled policy eats at the soul.' This is true of the Church. If all the time we are planning for retreat; to draw back to strong points which can be defended for just a little while longer, intending that the last man should die holding the flag aloft, then we are definitely going in the wrong direction. It may sound heroic that we are willing to defend the cause to the last, but it goes against the expectation of Jesus that the kingdom of heaven is going to 'forcefully advance' [Mt 11:12]. In Aberystwyth, we are planning to succeed.

We have been blessed by some significant movements in the strategic thinking of Christians across the world, as well as the new workings of the Spirit of God in many places at home and abroad. Interestingly, some two years before the Willow Creek Community Church had been heard about in Britain, I received a 'prophetic word' from Joyce Wallace, our churchwarden's wife. It was, 'When you get the invitation to visit Chicago, you are to go there.' I thought that it was a bit whacky, but kept the note in my pending tray for a while until, finally, I threw it away, thinking that this was just another one of those 'words' which came to nothing. It was not until a couple of years later that I was offered the chance to go to Toronto to see what was happening there, and I was also given enough money for a flight to Chicago to visit the Willow Creek Community church for a weekend. I apologised to Joyce and went.

In Toronto, I saw the Lord reaching people through the heart to the mind as they were touched by the Spirit, and then went away to reflect on what he was doing in their lives. Literally hundreds were falling under the impact of the Spirit on their lives as the Toronto Blessing was in full flow. In Willow Creek, I saw the Lord reaching people through the mind to the heart, as they were challenged to think about the Christian faith and examine it and see how relevant it was, and then to apply it to their hearts. The church had stripped down the normal worship service to a presentation style, where people are invited to participate at a level where they will not be compromised by making statements of faith which they do not believe, or join in prayers of confession when they have no understanding of the holiness of God nor feelings of repentance. It occurred to me that if these two approaches could be combined into one, then any church which took that as its basic approach to ministry would flourish. We aim to be one of those churches.

In addition to establishing 'Seeker Services' of our own, and regularly offering prayer ministry at the end of every public service, we have now set in motion a transformation of the house groups into cell groups, and that is still in the process of happening. Again, through the generosity of St. Michael's, my wife and I had the opportunity to visit Seoul, Korea in 1997. Amongst the benefits was an experience of their cell groups system. The thing which particularly impressed me was that their leaders are commissioned with the winning of a family to Christ every six months. If they fail, then they are 'punished' with a period of prayer and fasting, until the Lord answers their prayers for fruitfulness. What a way to get a congregation focused.

Because our churches are aimless, we never know whether we are making progress or not. We have so little to rejoice in, because we cannot say that we have reached our targets—for we have none. The thrill of seeing people coming to faith should keep us on the edge of our seats and should keep the whole congregation alert. Chrysostom's comment that 'I cannot believe in the salvation of anyone who does not work for the salvation of others' helps to keep us focused, as does J.C. Ryle's words that, 'The highest form of selfishness is that of the man who is content to go to heaven alone.'

After we shared this vision with the church on our return from Korea, our house groups immediately multiplied from seventeen to twenty three, and now number twenty five. We agreed, after several meetings and lengthy debate, that in the autumn of the following year we would start with a blank sheet of paper, intentionally restructuring our groups so that they would work on a more regional basis and would be specifically commissioned to 'multiply to grow'. There are some challenging statistics which go with this new strategy, indicating that if a group has not multiplied within two years there is a 95% chance that it will never do so. The gauntlet has been thrown down.

The 'tyranny of the volunteer' is a well known problem for churches, in common with many other human organizations. Volunteers come and go as they please. They mostly want their own way because they are giving their time free, and if they don't get it then they will leave. The standard of their work may not be up to much but woe betide anyone who tells them so. Because they are volunteers, if they do not like the way that things are going then they simply withdraw their commitment.

It is a very dangerous thing to 'professionalise' a church because it can quickly lead to a passenger mentality amongst the congregation. If there is a large paid staff, the feeling easily grows that the talents and gifts of the ordinary members are not needed any more, and they are free to get on with their own interests, so that they are actually less committed and involved than they have ever been. When any particular task arises which needs to be performed then the members can retreat into: 'We're paying people good money to do this for us. They should get on with it.'

Walking the tight-rope of increasing the number of paid staff in a parish contains many dangers, but because so many families now need both parents to be wage earners there are fewer and fewer volunteers to call on. Moreover, it is obvious that for some families and people in careers there are seasons when they cannot be involved to the same extent. Creating a guilt complex in them about their 'lack of commitment' is an ungracious and unfair thing to do. However, researchers have produced a convincing case that one clergyman can only look after about one hundred people. After that, as many people leave the church as join it if he tries to pastor the congregation all on his own. He will be putting new converts in at one end and the discouraged and neglected will be falling out at the other end. The 'revolving door' syndrome will be lived out in front of his eyes.

We have had to grasp this nettle in Aberystwyth, and have made a policy decision to invest in paid staff. We are now a team of fourteen full time with three part timers. This covers the ministry to the four churches of the parish, and includes five full time ordained clergy as well as lay pastoral assistants and administrative staff. We are called the 'Diocese of Aberystwyth' by those who want to have a go at us, but we are more interested in breaking growth barriers than answering our critics.

The tension which this has created in me is still unresolved. It requires trusting other colleagues to do work which by instinct I would prefer to do myself. It means retreating from the front line of pastoral contact; handing over some of the things I love like the Alpha work and, like a teacher become headmaster, retreating one step from the front line work. I am often reluctant to delegate, finding it hard to do so —simply because I love the work of the ministry so much.

One of the most welcome initiatives in Wales in recent years has been the establishment of the St.Teilo Trust, founded by Patrick Mansel Lewis. The trust exists to help fund and resource evangelism, exclusively in Wales. Initially, grants were given to various churches and parishes which were engaged in campaigns and projects, but as one of the early trustees I was pressing Patrick and other members of the board that we should look towards funding a bilingual evangelist for Wales. This was something that had been on my heart for some time.

After the trust had been functioning for a couple of years, Patrick quite unexpectedly approached me with the proposal that I should be the answer to my own prayers, and that I should take on evangelistic projects whilst continuing to be Rector of Aberystwyth. There was a lot of sense in the proposal, as Aberystwyth is so central to the rest of Wales. Some of us even think that it should be the capital of the Principality instead of Cardiff, but we don't get much support for our ideas! We can easily reach every corner of Wales in a couple of hours, and we already have a strong nucleus of Christians who could be involved in faith-sharing projects of various kinds. A further good reason for agreeing to Patrick's invitation was that with our large staff I could be away from the parish for a number of weeks each year without it having a substantial impact on the life of the churches.

It has always been said that, 'the need doesn't constitute a call', but it is hard to pray and long for something over a number of years and then when offered the opportunity to be involved in making that prayer into a reality actually turning it down. Consequently, in 1995 the parish of Aberystwyth agreed to release me for ten weeks a year to engage in front line evangelism wherever we were invited to take teams. This has become a regular part of our parish life and now involves more than just myself. Other members of staff are also taking teams away with them to help all kinds of evangelistic initiatives.

The value of this to Aberystwyth has been enormous. Originally we thought of ourselves as the 'giving parish', but it is now a regular pattern of our going out that we bring reports back to the congregation of how things have gone, what we have been involved in and how we have benefited. The result has been a congregation of people who have been growing in their own maturity and confidence through sharing their faith with others, and a further number of people who have grown in their intercessory ministry. We have sometimes actually taken an intercessory team with us to pray whilst others evangelise.

A few years ago, I was reading *The Power of Vision* by George Barna and was challenged to put into a sentence the vision that I had for my life and ministry. I am never any good at those sort of things because it all seems so self-conscious, but as I was reading and thinking, for once I had some inspiration and 'Recovering His Reputation' was a theme which seemed to get mental assent from me every way I looked at it.

On one of our evangelistic forays, in another part of Wales, we walked through a village on the way to the local church and we had to pass the pub. The door was open, and through the door came a blast of warm air, the sound of laughter and animated conversation. The building was well painted, and there was an obvious welcome on offer to all who went in. Then we came to the church. As the door opened we were greeted by a blast of cold air. Everyone inside was still wearing their overcoats and for a good reason—it was freezing. The smell in the air was musty and damp. The walls were covered in peeling paint and there was as much welcome as a refrigerator offers. The contrast was stark.

Whenever the Christian faith is represented by the media, it is almost always rubbished. The reputation of the church and of the Lord to whom we belong is at a very low ebb. We are seen as old-fashioned and irrelevant. Buildings are decaying. Only the elderly attend them. No-one with any intelligence believes the Christian faith any more; not even Christians themselves—and a parade of liberals and heretics is brought to the attention of the public, in order to discredit us further.

Our task in Aberystwyth is to 'recover His reputation', and our values reflect that. As the non-Christian world expects that our buildings will be decaying, we are going to ensure that they are in good repair. As they expect that our buildings will have peeling paint all over them, we will ensure that they are fresh and colourful. As they expect that we will have displays begging for money on all sides, we will make sure that our collections are as unobtrusive as possible. As they expect that the building will be almost empty when they come in, we are praying and working towards 'standing room only'. As they never expect to be welcomed or greeted, we will ensure that they can neither get in nor get out of the building without someone taking an interest in them. As they expect that the proceedings will be old fashioned, we are determined to ensure that we are contemporary in language and music. As they expect that all of it will be irrelevant, we will work at it to ensure that the relevance of our faith is clearly proclaimed. As they expect that all that we do will be dull and uninteresting, we are committed to ensure that it is bright and attractive.

As they have come to believe that everyone who goes to church is a hypocrite, we are determined to live down that image. As they believe that there is more love in the pub, we are going to show them that there is more love in the church than anywhere else on earth—and that this is the one place where they will be accepted uncritically.

A friend who had sung on the stage of Sadlers Wells said that, when a singer is in the midst of his performance, then he must make sure that it is his very best, because there are ten other people on stage with him thinking, 'I could do better than that'. This is the level of competition that many people experience outside the church. Another friend who came out of the gay community, when asked if they had pursued him, and tried to get him back, commented that they neither phoned nor called. The same was said by a man who had spent a large proportion of several years in the pubs of town. This is the level of real love which is experienced outside the church—not a lot.

We are charged by the Lord with producing a Christian community which expresses the one thing which will make the non-Christian world sit up and take notice—love. It is by the quality of our love that all people will know that we are His disciples. By the quality of our love for Him, and the quality of our love for others, we will 'recover His reputation' in Aberystwyth and throughout Wales.

The Fragrance of His Presence

PATRICK RILEY
Vicar of Glastonbury

My preparation for ordination took a quarter of a century. I was born in 1939 to the sound of war, and from then on I glimpsed the wonder of self-sacrificing love in the care everyone took of one another in the repeated bombing raids. This was in the south of London, so there was a great deal of coming and going of bombers and fighters and, inevitably, much confusion and destruction. I loved the impromptu parties in our large air-raid shelter. My father would go out when the air-raid siren wailed at the beginning of a raid, and bring in anyone caught on their way to the local hospital, which was just up the road from the family home. Cataracts of love, a corporate life, and endless cups of tea! A child has such a straightforward understanding of life, and for me the fragility of bodies and homes and buildings was not as central or important as the overwhelming unity which came from being aware that everyone was in it together, and that therefore nothing else really mattered. A deep sense of unity between individuals was my first inkling of the love of God in action. With the outbreak of peace in 1945, there came what, for me, was an unqualified disaster. The wartime closeness with neighbours evaporated, and people seemed to want to concentrate on their own lives, to the exclusion of others. What a loss! As a child I knew that something valuable was missing and, as I grew up, I began to see that there was a pattern of first getting a glimpse of the glory of love in action, then experiencing the gradual failure to appreciate such love, and thus seeing the death of the original drive and power. The vision would fade, and only an empty shell would remain.

During this time there was worship with the family in the local parish church in all the wonder of the full Anglo-Catholic faith. This meant

61

services resplendent in drama, music and sacramental extravagance, 'bells and smells', and a sense of the numinous which pervaded even the simplest act of worship. That was when the idea of ordination to the priesthood seemed to me an inevitable, and also utterly daunting, possibility. Later, I encountered local house-parties of Mirfield monks, where the outpourings of love and compassion, with the strength of a joyful discipline, moulded my longings to serve as an ordinary parish priest. Quite outstanding priests from the diocese of Southwark joined in, and turned ordinary meetings into life-changing experiences. It was about the time of the foundation of the Southwark Ordination scheme, which seemed very 'modern' to many people, but which we tended to regard as the most obvious and rewarding idea, because it was 'local' (in a farmhouse across some fields) and because we knew, loved and respected those who were leading it. There was new life, new thinking, and it was good to be part of it.

Elsewhere, there were other responses to the miseries and wastefulness of war. Chiara Lubich had begun what became a movement of unity during the war in Italy, and this grew out of the feeling of helplessness in the face of such huge international conflict. I learnt that the Focalare Movement, as it was called, concentrated on living the Gospel, in simplicity, daily. Such was the impact of this amazingly simple rule that spread widely. Large gatherings took place each year where, with new songs and excellent teaching and sharing, the life of faith came alive in a new way. The movement spread to this country soon after the war, and by the late 1950s had been the vehicle for a new understanding of unity between Roman Catholics, the Church of England and the other churches. People were meeting one another with a new humility, and regarding themselves primarily as Christians, not simply defenders of a denomination. As I became involved, I discovered that God need not be defended either. The Spirit recognises Spirit, and the unity which flowed from these meetings further energised the church in which I grew up. There were also day meetings, and I well remember one held in Twickenham. Hundreds of people were present, most of whom we had never met, but within a very short time there was a lovely, lively unity. It was as if you met again old family friends, and the warmth of recognition was a joy shared. This corporate intimacy is always an indicator to me of the love of God in action. The life of the Spirit is not to be grasped, labelled and contained, but is glimpsed from the corner of an eye, and seen moving away elsewhere like that lovely image in

Exodus 33, where Moses is protected from the full vision of God's power, and is given just the back view after God has passed by. The truth is seen and known by these elusive pictures, like a fragrance, or the sound of a bell reverberating in still air. By such delicate images God makes Himself known in gentleness, lest the fullness of His love be too much for us at present.

After five years of training at Leeds University and Mirfield, there followed ordination (and marriage — what an amazing double sacrament) and Elizabeth and I were launched into a classic Anglo-Catholic parish, with a classic Anglo-Catholic training Vicar, and I can remember distinctly the feeling that now a new response to God's overwhelming love could really begin in me, and in the new parish I was called to serve.

It took some time for me to realise that we can overestimate God's need for our guidance and that, in fact, most people overestimate their spirituality, their sense of humour and their ability to drive! The vision became clouded in a big way. The Focalare Movement, which had been such a lively place of expression, for me became dulled. I missed my old friends who somehow moved the church forward with the love they shared. It was nearly always fascinating to be with them, and occasionally it was quite breathtakingly good. But now the Focalarini that I met seemed caught up in the 'churchiness' of the movement. What was originally the vehicle for unity, the songs and the lifestyle of seeing Jesus in everyone that one met, became an end in itself. It was as if the life had gone out of the movement for me. I am sure the movement continued, and still continues, to inspire and encourage, but for me there was something missing.

About this time, there was much talk of unity with the Methodist Church, and this seemed such a good and natural fulfilment of a deep longing that the local churches had experienced. The effect of the failure of the unity scheme on a young and green curate was predictable. The great hopes for a new way forward for the churches, acting locally, could not withstand the chilling hand of the church acting nationally. At least that was how it felt then, and the result was a deep sadness. At about the same time that the Anglican-Methodist discussions failed, countless projects and ideas in the daily life of the parish failed. Mistakes were made, and unwise pastoral decisions caused the sort of difficulties that most parishes have. Suddenly, all was dry and dull. In this situation it is not surprising that depression lurked. There is a limit to the dissonance which humans can tolerate, and the obvious way out presented itself. I reckoned that a life which was carefully structured, and yet did not deliver the goods of contentment, fulfilment and joy to me personally, clearly was not structured enough. The control of a strict discipline was clearly not working, therefore more of the same must be needed. It was a natural mistake made by someone who needed at that time to fly, to control his situation in his endeavours to find freedom.

It seemed that a God-given faith had become a man-made religion. Instead of being enlarged in vision and in the capacity to love, which is the gift of faith, there was a diminution of my understanding, so that the outworkings of a living faith became a replacement for the experience itself. There is nothing new here, but this development of a private idol, especially a 'religious' one, is difficult to discern, and can be so easy to live with, and so comfortable to draw round the daily hurts and feelings of worthlessness. It is nevertheless a fake, and like all fakes leads us astray. For me, it meant an unbearable (and literally so, for everyone else) longing for a perfection which in all reality cannot be gained this side of the grave, but which can become a most destructive monster. It can demand and expect a completeness and satisfaction in relationships which is quite unrealistic, and yet when it is not attained, leads to a resentment towards others, and a sense of failure in oneself. Perfection itself can become a secondary terrible idol. We should expect others—and ourselves—to be sinners, albeit forgiven sinners! To expect perfection from anyone, including ourselves, is to crush them.

Nevertheless, although my inner life was becoming sterile, outwardly my life exhibited energy, drive and an enthusiasm that was dependent on theory rather than experience. I was busting a gut to energise our church, but without considering whose church it was, and is. The long curacy ended, and I was invited to move to another part of Somerset to serve five small parishes which were destined to become one parish legally. What an opportunity! Within a few years, with my drive and energy, I was having a marvellous time. All sorts of united ventures were begun; the parishes even shared their finances as well as their buildings! There were Bible study groups, sermon preparation groups and after-school clubs, and all the evidence of life, and yet—and yet, and yet. It was as if we had painstakingly designed and built the most marvellous jumbo jet which could easily accommodate us all, and had driven it up and down the runway, endlessly, saying all the time what a joy it was to be flying, and yet never actually taking off. Becoming a

Rural Dean did nothing to help my deepest longings for a renewed life in the Spirit, for at one time amongst the twenty five or so parishes in the deanery, there were seventeen parishes without clergy. The daily care of them was my responsibility. Imagine trying to design and build seventeen jumbo jets all at once—never mind feeling duty bound to fly them all. That was how it felt. The frenetic activity which resulted was good for no-one. Yet the tender trap, developed by me, personally, was closing, and my family and those who loved me, and even my spiritual director, could not help me see what was happening. This was the reason that I did not have the time nor the energy to see that my dear wife, Elizabeth, was becoming ill. For a long time it was not diagnosed by the doctors that she had a failed thyroid gland, pernicious anaemia and arthritis. We just assumed that it was middle age taking its toll, and that was why we both felt very weary most of the time. Little did we understand the different causes of our tiredness.

As part of the preparation for a visit by Colin Urquhart to the nearby town of Frome, all the local clergy were sent invitations. Because I was too busy, I had not thought to go, but Elizabeth was talking with our doctor, who suggested that it might be helpful, so she went. All she asked for, during the time of ministry, was for peace of mind. Her healing began. I could see the difference in her daily increase of energy and sparkle, the joy in her eyes and the opening out of her loving to me and to the whole family. She began to read the Bible with an expectancy and excitement, and her prayer times (we have always prayed separately) were obviously enormously enriching and empowering. In short, she came alive in a new way.

This should have filled me with the greatest joy. Instead, I was plunged into a deep depression. What was happening to my best friend? Was this normal? Was it healthy, or was it a huge fantasy that would explode in a decidedly messy way in a very short time? Here was I, with a longing to find again those glimpses of glory which I knew to be real, yet which I could see neither in the Church at that time nor in my own life, where 'mustage and oughtery' grew without let or hindrance. Yet here was Elizabeth, with no great striving and strain, healed in a big way. The arthritis and the failed thyroid had severely limited her life, but now she was well and free. I could not see this at all. Apart from anything else it was all so unfair. I was slogging my heart out and getting nowhere, and she was just sitting there, well and grinning. I dropped deeper into depression as I tried to fathom what God was doing.

Bishop Morris Maddocks had just been appointed as the Diocesan Healing Advisor, and he was helping many people come to understand what God was doing in His church in this generation in the ministry of healing. His stature, wisdom and depth of prayer assisted me to begin afresh the search for a new wholeness in my ministry.

That new start was encouraged by the invitation by the Bishop to go and serve another group of five parishes around Glastonbury, which was renowned as an ancient Christian site, and a place of pilgrimage, and a growing New Age centre, where, I had heard, it was confidently asserted that all spiritually inclined people had both feet planted firmly in the clouds.

The move and the new horizons, the listening and discerning, absorbed all my energies, so the questions about renewal and healing were put in with all the other things needing assessment. There they stayed, until I got a hefty shove, to encourage me to re-think, and which began a time of great release which had the fragrance and the quiet reverberation which I had begun to recognise as the experience of God-in-action, the Holy Spirit.

After a weekend course on the ministry of healing, held at Abbey House (the Diocesan Retreat house in the parish), there was such a huge response that the leader asked if he could use the parish church for the final service. This was an outstanding occasion, and afterwards the elderly churchwarden simply said, 'We must have more of this, Vicar.' So we did. This was the first big change for me: a major turning-point. Here was a movement of God not asked for by me, and not organised by me, and far more powerful than anything I had experienced before.

The sovereign God could manage without me in charge! What a good lesson to learn. That was only the beginning of a whole new way of living and loving God's Word-in-action, experiencing the work of the Holy Spirit in a new way. All the blessings of shared ministry then began to flow. It happened that the *Saints Alive* course had been a bit of a heavy 'ought', and I was not looking forward to the follow-up, but part of the group who had been to the first *Saints Alive* volunteered to lead the second one and, furthermore, were prepared to spend time praying, visiting and working, to make this excellent course a real focus for renewal in the church. You could almost hear the chains falling off, such was my relief at being shown an obvious new way (for me) of releasing gifts in others by removing the Vicarial hand. I had always rejoiced in a fairly high level of delegation, but I now saw that that was only within the context of the Vicar having the power of veto. There was no doubt as to who was in control, however many people offered help. As a result of this deeper letting-go, prayer groups, study groups, renewal groups all began to flourish. One in particular grew to such an extent that they had to meet in the back of church, because the homes were not big enough to take the numbers that wanted to join in. The signs of God at work were being recognised by more and more people. The fragrance of the Lord's presence — our sense of the Holy Spirit at work among us — ensured that we all paid a deep attention to what He was doing. Members of prayer groups from miles away would come and be refreshed. The best thing of all was that this was not the result of clever preaching, nor brilliant advertising; we were simply overtaken and overwhelmed in simplicity and joy. I began to experience the love of God in a new way, but without any clear 'moment' of transition. It was as if I had begun a new part of my journey with new zest and hopefulness; the same journey, but travelling in a new way.

The 'Toronto' experience followed. Many from the parish went, and again found that 'first love' renewed with joy and hope. They returned and gave it all away to those of us who did not go transatlantic. This was the time of a cataract of grace; an absolute Niagara of unmerited favour, which released me and so many others in the church into a new world. There were now words from the Lord, tongues and interpretations, and some prophetic gifts. The key factor here seemed to be the non-possessive love which encourages a corporate intimacy: Kingdom living. I had glimpsed this so many times, and so often missed, dropped, or otherwise lost, this loving. Yet here, as undeserved gift, came the gentle and powerful reality of all that I had learned, preached and taught for a quarter of a century.

God became a beckoning Word. The daily office and the Eucharist became places to meet the living God, personally. Times of prayer before public worship became full of wonder and meaning. The worship itself, shared with so many others who were beginning to come alive to the promise and presence of God, really took off. (How could we have existed with such unprepared and unrehearsed and totally insipid worship?)

What had I been doing all those years? Was it all just a preparation for this? How had I been satisfied with 'religion' when, all the time, 'revelation' had been awaiting me? I now understood why I had always remembered the saying of the small child, during a sermon, proclaimed in the piercing whisper that only a child can achieve: 'When the Vicar stops talking, we are going to see God.'

I was so amazed by what God was doing through 'my' ministry, (which was actually the ministry of many), that I was unprepared for what God was preparing to do in me personally. I have occasionally received a word from God which has had the fragrance of the Real Thing, and which has been confirmed by others. One instance of this occurred when I was particularly caught up with an over-full timetable of urgent and, in themselves, quite proper, events. I heard a voice which (in the sense that God had just that moment passed by) just said, 'All diaries are mine. Your diary is my diary. You will be blessed in your care of it.' On another occasion I dreamed I was digging in a beautiful walled garden, but was filled with anxiety in case I dug up an unexploded bomb. In the dream, I then heard a voice say to me, 'Yes, there is an unexploded bomb, and when you come across it, put it by the hedge near the wall, and I will deal with it later. You just get on with the digging.' Needless to say, the anxiety left. I was able to continue the parish work, when I woke up, without any further worries. After these sorts of words and dreams, I was totally unprepared for what God offered next. This time it was not simply a word, but an offer, and with a choice attached to it.

I had smoked a pipe for many years, enjoying the comfort and the habit enormously. At the age of sixteen I had been presented by my father with my first hand-crafted pipe, which had been made by skilled pipemakers in London, and I began a collection of pipes which were all rigorously, regularly (and frequently) tested. I was then part of a very British, Manly, and Sophisticated group. This was what I thought at the time, along with many others. When, over the years, the others wisely gave up smoking, I too tried to give up, many, many times, but without success. Years later, I was still trying to give up and yet, at the same time, was glad that I had not succeeded in doing so. The futility of such an attitude was obvious and irritating. The habit was also very expensive, quite apart from the discomfort and danger to my family and friends. During a time of prayer at one of our evening services, I had asked for prayer because I was feeling so tired. While some dear friends surrounded me with loving attention and deep prayerful support, I again had the experience of having just heard God speak clearly. What He said was, 'I will deal with the compulsion, but you must deal with

68

the addiction.' This was an offer that required a response. It was not some 'nice' vision, or a vaguely comforting feeling; this was at the very meeting place with the living God. This was holy ground. I could either go on as before, refusing to change, or I could accept the gift of freedom from the compulsion (whatever that was), and also accept the decision to fight the addiction to nicotine. Now there was a stunner of an offer. In thinking through how I could explain such a powerful word and offer, a picture came to me. In it, I was standing astride two railway trucks, a foot on each, looking down at the coupling below as the train rushes along the track. In a second, the coupling breaks, and the two parts of the train begin to pull apart. I have to make a decision fast if I am to survive in one piece—literally. Do I accept the power of the locomotive and jump towards the engine, or do I jump so as to stay with the trucks, knowing that there is no power, and that they will eventually grind to a standstill? This described the inner tension that followed the word and offer to me from God.

I am glad to say that two years later I am still enjoying freedom from the addiction, although there are times it still makes the old appeal (so far, unsuccessfully) —perhaps from force of habit, or when I am tired. I am sure that this victory is not due to any personal strength of my own, but has happened because the compulsion has been removed. The bomb of fear has been located and, as instructed, placed out of the way. For this I give thanks daily, telling anyone who will listen that the healing God gives is not always understood fully, often having to do with parts of our being which are deeply hidden from ourselves, but not from Him.

For so many years I had tried to serve God, who had somehow to be contained within my comprehension. If I could not understand with my mind, then I did not want to commit myself. I had wanted to remain in a position of 'safety'. I needed to be opened up to the wonder of God, greater than my wildest dreams, more than I could ever understand. I needed to obey, in faith, in order to understand. In spite of all the longing, and the real desire to live by faith, not works, the reality was that I was only prepared to live, so to speak, an internal and self-validating faith. Gradually, my faith has been extended and enlarged as a pure gift of God. To put it another way, I have begun to live by passive volition and not by active volition. I am now beginning to be drawn into the existence of Glory, and self-forgetting delight, instead of striving for a cerebral kingdom of my own invention.

SERVANTS OF THE LIVING GOD

Perhaps only a poem can begin to explain the change in my life.

THE HARBOUR

I stood on the harbour wall
and watched the setting sun
in various hues of shepherd's delight.
A glorious, soul-raising, breathtaking sight.

'All that I am I give to Thee,
and all that I have I commit to Thee.
Put me with whom you will, dear Father.
Love of my love, you are all to me.'

Such was my prayer to the Infinite.

It seemed such a long way to pray,
'til I heard a voice at my feet -
a smiling Christ, in a boat, I heard say,

'Patrick, all that I am I give thee,
and all that I have I commit to thee.
Put Me with whom you will, dear brother,
Love of My Love, you are all to Me.'

And I set sail that day.

Give *Him* the Glory

NEIL COHEN
Rector of Christ Church, Jerusalem

I am six feet tall and in 1983 I was fit and strong: well, fitter and stronger than I am now that I am quite a few years older. Yet strong as I was, I could not force my way to my feet. I was pinned down on my knees, feeling both helpless and very foolish indeed.

It was a sultry October evening, St. Luke's Day, and I was in a strange church, not even in my diocese. It had been a long sequence of events that had brought me to this point and over most of them I had no control. I was new to the ordained ministry, having been priested just sixteen months previously. A 'born-again' Christian from the church in which I was serving as curate had been 'pestering' me, telling me again and again that a dimension was missing from the ministry I was exercising.

'What a cheek', I thought, full of my new found authority as a clergyman. I was not only a new priest, but also a new Christian, so it was, perhaps, not surprising that this had been my reaction. Though I had been born a Jew, it was a surprise to me that God had called me into the full-time ministry of the Church of England. My Jewish relatives had not been *surprised*—that is simply not a strong enough word to convey the shock, sense of betrayal and disappointment that I had turned my back on my heritage. They could not understand that I was not denying my Jewishness. Since Jesus and his disciples and first generation of followers were Jewish, I was actually fulfilling my heritage as a Jew by accepting him as Lord.

So how had I reached this point in my life, at which I was about to experience the amazing renewing power of the Holy Spirit, in a new way? The story is one that I happily recount, so as to encourage others.

The road to ordination had been long and hard, and perhaps more than a little unusual. Not only was there my Jewish background, but when I felt God calling me to the ministry I was a thirty year old without academic qualifications. My first twenty years had certainly been difficult ones, but the Lord intervened—to put right many things that were not in accordance with His will; to call me to serve Him in full-time Christian ministry; and to show me the vital significance of my Jewishness.

Ours had not been an observant family. After his Bar Mitzvah, Dad had decided that God was not a reality for him, so our home was totally devoid of all religious influence. My sister and I were sent to the local (Church of England) infants' school. Immediately, we were thrown into the turmoil of religious intolerance. Excluded from assemblies and religious instruction, we had to sit in the corridor while these activities were going on.

There was some contact with the church as I grew up. I joined the Cubs attached to our local parish church. Discovering that the church choristers were paid for their services, I joined up in order to earn some pocket money —singing at countless weddings, and for Sunday services, for my two shillings a month. No objection was raised at home. At least it kept me away from Dad, with whom I had a very poor relationship. My father had been through the horrors of the Second World War as a regular soldier, receiving injuries in the campaigns he fought in; some of those injuries were emotional. He had had to endure abuse from his comrades in arms, simply because he was a Jew— 'It's all your fault Cohen, that we are in this war; your people have caused it.' Because of that, and because there was a real fear that at some point the Germans would invade England, Dad changed our family name from Cohen to Cornell. (More recently, I have changed back to Cohen.) The problem now was that he had been called up as a reservist to fight in the Korean war, when I was only four years old, not returning for the next five years. By this time, I was the 'man of the house' and so resented his invasion of 'my' space. Of course that is not the way I spoke at the time, but it is certainly how I felt as a young child.

The 'eleven plus' examination was good for me. I was bright enough to do well without a great deal of effort, winning a scholarship to a minor public school. Considerable merit points were won from Dad for that, but our relationship was strained all the time. When I was sent home—permanently—after just four terms, the relationship worsened. His anger would erupt at any moment, and I bore the brunt of it.

Determined to leave home at the earliest possibility, I signed up with the Royal Artillery band as a Junior Musician, at the age of fifteen years and two months. My antisocial behaviour took on a new dimension. I had discovered at school that having money in one's pocket was a sure way to have friends around one. Now I made the mistake of stealing from the very people I was wanting to befriend. When the civil police were called into our barracks, I could not cope with the thought of being exposed as the culprit.

A rusty razor blade seemed to offer me a way out, but I was ignorant about human physiology, slashing too high up my wrists, so only succeeded in losing a lot of blood, and passing out. I awoke to find myself in the military hospital at Woolwich. I was subsequently given a medical discharge from the army.

My mother and sister supported me as best as they could, but to all intents and purposes I felt totally alone in the world, with no friends, no future, no hope. Still only eighteen years old, my life seemed to me to be utterly pointless. Of course, I blamed anyone and everyone for my situation. Deciding to travel, I took off for France, and a new journey of exploration into myself. I was yet to discover who I was and what the purpose of my life might be. A succession of jobs followed and I met and fell in love with Fran, whom I was to marry. Then, through a 'Folk Service' that I attended as a member of the Hammersmith Folk Club, I encountered Father Ken Loveless, then Rural Dean of Hackney, East London, who was preaching at the event. An extreme Anglo-Catholic priest, he might not have been thought the 'ideal' sort of friend for me; I would never have chosen him as such. Yet he saw in me something which I had never seen—potential. He offered me a new kind of future, one in which God figured. Although I did not actually believe in God, Ken was persuasive! He had a vision for me.

Ken had given me his card and one day, unable to settle to my work, I dialled his number. The telephone conversation went like this:

'Hackney Deanery. Father Loveless speaking.'

'Ah, Ken.... I was wondering....'

'Neil, dear boy, I am free this evening at 9.00 p.m. I shall see you then.' And the phone went dead.

I had been summoned to Hackney Deanery, and I did not want to go. When five o'clock came and work was over for the day, Fran and I found our way by tube to Hackney station. We wandered around, looking for Broke Road. Hackney was being rebuilt and street after street was devoid of housing. One very grand house stood on a corner and proved to be the rectory. Ken lived in splendid isolation in this Victorian building which had at least five storeys, including a cellar and an attic! We wandered around until nine, then ascended the steps to the front door.

Ken answered the bell immediately. 'Make your way up the stairs as far as you can go, and wait for me there.' Fran was shown into the sitting room and told to wait! When Ken says something you do it. He had been a Lieutenant Commander in the Royal Navy!

At the top of the stairs, as far as I could go, was an attic room which had been converted into a private chapel. An altar, a prie-dieu, icons and candles by the score—and no-one else. I entered the chapel and waited—it was only a couple of minutes, but when Ken entered it could have been the Pope or the Vicar of Bray, for all I knew. The biretta was on his head and he wore a lace cotta and a beautiful French silk priest's stole.

'On your knees, boy, and tell God all about it!'

I was not given a chance to protest that I did not believe in God. This was Commander Loveless speaking. Kneeling at the prie-dieu, I started to speak into the emptiness. As far as I knew, I was addressing the ether. As I spoke, I began to pour out my heart. I was on my knees, not knowing whether anyone other than Ken could hear me, but out it all poured, like bile! All the bitterness, the rage, the anger, disappointment and shame; the sense of being useless and unloved, unlovable and unlovely.... It all came flooding out in an unstoppable deluge. I cried, I sobbed, I screamed. I blew my nose repeatedly (using a box of tissues located strategically nearby.) I fell face down on the floor. Banging my fists in rage and frustration, I was a child who had suddenly found the means of communicating the feelings that had been inside. Nothing was going to stop me until I ran out of things to say, feelings to wring out of myself—having exhausted all that had been building up in me for over twenty years. All the while, Ken had stood quietly by, listening.

Eventually, I stopped. I dried up, both literally—my eyes and nose— and metaphorically. I had said it all. Ken gently placed his hands on my head, praying for God's absolution. Then he gave me a blessing.

How can I describe the feeling that flooded through me as I received an absolution and blessing, given in God's name. Words cannot describe it. It is at such a moment that we recognise the futility of our hopelessly inadequate language. As Ken used the words, 'By the authority vested in me as a priest of the Church...' it was as if I were standing under a shower—not just cleansing the outside, but somehow permeating the whole of my being. As the words of the absolution rang in my ears, I began to feel clean from the inside out. I had never felt like this before. It was a wonderful experience which somehow, in my confusion, I wanted to last for ever. I still did not understand or believe in God. Yet God was clearly dealing with me, through Ken that night. God understood me. God believed in me. 'The peace of God which passeth all understanding....' I began to know that inward peace.

When we went downstairs to join Fran in Ken's sitting room, I felt like a new person, though I could not begin to understand then what had just happened in the chapel. There was only the feeling of cleanness, inner peace and a strange sense of not feeling guilty any longer, which convinced me that I had not imagined it all.

Over Ken's fine Glenfiddich single malt twelve year old whisky, he explained something of what had taken place. He talked about God in a way which, not surprisingly, I had never heard of before—as a friend; as a benign Lord who had no hatred toward anyone in His heart, and no room in His kingdom for anyone with hatred in their heart, no matter whom it was directed against or for what reason. We talked through the night and got to know each other. I would still have been there for lunch if I had not remembered that soon I must take Fran back to her flat and make my own way back to Putney for a clean shirt and a new day at the bank where I was working.

As Fran and I walked down the stairs from the rectory door, I was a different young man from the one who had walked up them the previous evening. To my astonishment, Ken called after me, 'I'll see you ordained before I die.'

Some time later, hearing that Fran and I wished him to marry us, a delighted Ken commanded immediately, 'If I am to marry you it shall be in a church. You will need to get yourself baptised, Neil, and you may as well both be confirmed too.' (He had already discovered that Fran was baptised but not confirmed.)

To my local parish church I went, asking to be baptised. With virtually no preparation I was submitted to the water of baptism in December 1969. So it was that Fran and I began attending church together, were duly confirmed the following March and married soon afterwards.

The scene at the wedding was an extraordinary one. All the people on 'my side' of the church were, of course, Jewish. Most of them had never been into a church before in their lives. Father Ken stood before the congregation and said, 'This couple have been brought together by Christ, and have now been married in Christ's church.' Peering intently over his half glasses he continued, 'They will need all the help you heathens out there can give them!' A light and humorous touch, but perhaps open to misunderstanding!

Needless to say, that sermon did not endear him to my family! Actually, they were furious—but not for long. Two hours later, at the reception, he redeemed himself. It was not anything he said, but his contribution to the festivities which made all the difference. Fran and I, and indeed Ken, had originally met through our mutual passion for Folk Dance and song. I had been a Morris Man, and he sang sea shanties, and played the concertina. As this was a Morris Man's wedding, the tradition was for the groom to dance a solo Morris jig, which I duly did. Imagine the comical effect when Ken, still in his biretta and surplice, played the concertina for us. This was too much for my hitherto irate family. They roared with laughter at this strange figure, and Ken won the day.

The first time we went to the local church in the town to which we moved, we were welcomed like long lost friends. Very soon we got stuck in: PCC, choir, serving etc., etc. I'm sure you know how it is! A young couple move in and are enthusiastic, so you provide them with every possible opportunity to give of their energies.

After a few years, it became very clear that what Ken had said to me was not going to go away — ordination became a very clear and insistent option. After a long struggle against it, I went to see the vicar, to talk the matter over. Almost before I knew what was happening, I was being interviewed by the bishop and the Diocesan Director of Ordinands. Then I was sent off to another local clergyman who had been a tutor at one of the Theological colleges, to read some theology. I had to write some essays set by him, to prove that I had the necessary intellectual ability to follow a course of study.

What I wrote seemed to convince the bishop that there was some hope for me, so off I went to a selection conference. No-one had ever asked me if I knew that I was going to go to heaven, or if I was sure that Jesus is the Son of God. Perhaps it was all just assumed?

The two week wait after the ACCM conference went by slowly, but finally the letter came. The decision was: 'Yes .... But.' 'Yes', I was to be recommended for training for the full-time ordained ministry in the

Church of England; 'but' I must first complete two years on the Aston Training Scheme, a new pre-theological college course for people about whom ACCM had reservations.

Those two years were awful! The pressure that they put on my family life was intolerable, and we struggled our way through them. We made some good friends, and we learned a lot, but was it all worth the strain? In retrospect I have to say that as a means to an end it was but, as an experience in itself, it was not!

Having satisfied the requirements of the Advisory Council for the Church's Ministry, off we went to full-time theological college; two more years of study, essays and lectures, books, books, books. Ordination came in June 1980. To my intense astonishment, Dad came to the service. He had not come to our wedding, and he had ignored both myself and our children whenever we visited. But he came to act as navigator for mum, who had never been to Guildford before, and this ensured that he attended. (Happily, we were reconciled in later years.)

After more than two years as curate at Great Bookham, I had an experience of the Lord's power and love which I had previously read about, but had never thought necessary. On the renewing work of the Holy Spirit, I had taken my cue from my training vicar. He sincerely believed that the things of the Holy Spirit are an optional extra, for the less intellectually able. Understandably, therefore, I had not been seeking this for myself. I came into it by a series of circumstances quite outside of my control.

At Bookham I discovered that there were some 'born-again' Christians in the congregation. They mostly seemed at the time to be a 'nuisance' to the vicar and myself, but one of them had become a good friend, and kept inviting me, every month, to a meeting in another church. Each time I was asked, I had consistently been able to find some valid excuse not to go, until one month when she caught me off guard, and I had no excuse. So I went.

We arrived at the pretty little church, forty minutes drive away, which was to be the place where the Lord would move me forward, did I but know it. First, we launched into Evening Prayer. I had already said Evening Prayer that day, and was in any case present with very little good grace. I began to feel trapped into being somewhere I was not meant to be. When Evening Prayer was over, some gentle choruses were sung. It was at this point that I found myself on my knees, actually enjoying the sense of God's presence in a new way. It was the chorus *Spirit of the Living God, fall afresh on me* which got me. It gripped me. The words spoke to me in such a powerful way. I was literally rooted to the spot. Beginning to feel foolish, I tried to get up, aware that all around me people were standing to worship. I felt very exposed and vulnerable, and did not like those feelings at all.

I felt that I had become good at my work and had been finding a self-confidence which had never been there before. I had begun to receive letters of thanks after funerals, and liked the new sense of being appreciated. Not knowing how to handle it, I had taken pleasure in the letters, filing them neatly in alphabetical order in a special file. I received any form of affirmation greedily.

Now, on my knees, I became angry! This was certainly not what I had come to the service for. What I had come for I did not really know, but I was sure it was not to be humiliated!

The anger changed to frustration, and I began to weep—quietly. I was not about to attract further attention to myself in this position. After all, I was a priest and all the people around me were laity. I certainly could not let them see me as a weak person. Mercifully, *Spirit of the Living God* was the last chorus to be sung, so the pressure subsided as people began to sit down. I slunk to the back of the church—to observe from a safe distance. But I was not allowed to escape.

I did not want any more challenges tonight, thank you! It was then that some of the good folk there spotted me as I stood, back-to-the-wall. They came towards me. 'Neil, we want to pray for you.' I was *not* about to be prayed for by lay people. I was a priest. I was supposed to pray for them! But they propelled me into a pew, and started to pray in tongues for me to receive the Holy Spirit.

During the time of ministry, God spoke to me! It was the first time I had ever heard Him speak in such a clear way. There have been times since, but this was the first time, the most awesome. He knew that there was a real problem in me about pride. He also knew that the best way of dealing with this was to take away all my defences before He could address it. 'GIVE ME THE GLORY.' That is what He said to me. 'GIVE ME THE GLORY.' There was no doubt in my mind that He was referring to the file of thank-you letters that I had sorted neatly into alphabetical order. He said nothing more than 'give me the glory' at the time. That was enough. Was I really stealing the glory from God? That was the clear implication. I was devastated.

'Lord, I am sorry that I have taken the credit for all that you have accomplished in me. I really am sorry' was my prayer. Maybe there was more I could have said, but that seemed to be enough. For the moment I said it, the floodgates opened. I began to weep; not with shame or anger, but with a sense of relief and joy. There was a sense deep within me that a new relationship with God was about to begin, and I was glad—to the very core of my being.

Those praying for me encouraged me to pray in tongues myself. At first, the sounds that came were simply grunts, but they told me to persevere and that, after a time, a new vocabulary would come to me, for prayer and worship. They were right. I began to experience the power of the Holy Spirit, and the gifts of God, including the gift of tongues, in a new way. It was real.

Back in the parish, the next problem was whether I should tell my vicar what had happened. Was there a right way to do so? I knew that I was soon to move on to a new parish, but that move was still some months away. I still had to work day by day with my vicar, and he was sure to notice.

The Lord had all this in hand. I was booked into a week's leadership course at the Hyde, the centre of ministry for Colin Urquhart's Bethany Fellowship. Had I gone on that course without the experience I have just described, it would have had very little value. God's timing, as always, was impeccable. It was a renewal course, for renewal leaders in the Church. At the Hyde, I asked several members of staff, how I should tell my vicar what had happened. They all said the same thing. 'If he asks you, then ask him, "Do you really want to know?" If he then says "Yes", tell him. But if he says "No", don't; at least then you are putting the responsibility of knowledge onto him.' That made excellent sense, so when he did inevitably ask me what had happened to me, I asked, 'Do you really want to know?' He said 'Yes', so I told him, and it did not damage our relationship, as I had feared it might. At the conference I learned a good deal about salvation, and the assurance that we can have that we are saved—by grace, not by works, so that no man can boast. The teaching by Charles Sibthorpe, Bob Gordon and other members of the Bethany Fellowship was first class. This was Colin Urquhart's territory, and coming from where I had been, firmly in the liberal wing of the church, with little or no biblical understanding, it was all a bit of a culture shock; but the Lord had prepared me for it on St. Luke's Day. At the Hyde, I became aware for the first time that I was destined for heaven. Now that is what renewal is about! I was really born again. Now I knew—not *hoped* any more, but *knew*—that I was going to live with Jesus in his Kingdom for ever. For the first time, I said 'hallelujah' and meant it.

The ministry which God had entrusted to me had, until that turning-point in my life been carried out to *my* glory, and in *my* strength. The nett result had been praise and thanks to *me*. Now things were to change. I now knew that God could change lives. Only God could give me the power and use me, to enable that change to come about. Now I knew that only God deserved that glory and thanks, so it was for me to let Him go to work in me first. SURRENDER! How hard it was for me to do this. I had been forced by circumstances to become a hard person: hard on the outside and hard on the inside. I was really a 'loner' though by now married and a father.

Now I prayed *with* people, not just *for* them. Through the Holy Spirit I became aware of my own spiritual needs and gained a deepening understanding of others' needs, too. I began to see people converted. Before I was filled with the Spirit, I had no idea of the need for conversion. No-one had ever asked me about it. No-one had ever told me that it was necessary. No-one had asked me whether I was saved. Nor had I been taught how to bring anyone else to the Cross of Jesus Christ, for them to be saved.

Preaching became something very different. From arid, mind-searching excursions, the Lord now led me to speak about spiritual understanding and commitment, about faith, and confidence in Scripture. Worship became a joy, rather than just part of a liturgy. The Bible became Good News. Prayer became communication with a loving Father, more than a duty.

We moved on to our second parish in April 1984. St. Martin's, Old Dean was a second curacy. I was, in effect, priest in charge of a daughter church, on a council estate just outside Camberley in Surrey. I was to be the eighth curate in the twenty three years since the church had been founded.

We went there with a real sense of guidance from the Lord. Having had a prophecy about going there, while I was still an ordinand, our confidence was sky-high. The Archdeacon had asked me some months earlier what sort of parish I thought we should be looking for, and I had given him a list of ten criteria! He had shown some surprise, and had intimated that no such parish existed in the diocese, but that he would see what he could do. A week or so later, he telephoned to say that such a parish did in fact exist in the other archdeaconry. Would I consider having a look at it? Would I? Of course I would.

The first Sunday in Camberley was a revelation. I was the only man present! At Bookham we had seen over two hundred people at the Sunday service. Here there were just over forty. Clearly there was much to be done. Some of my predecessors had brought in two hundred plus to family services, so there was potential. But clergy had come and gone, so continuity and stability were lacking.

Before moving I was certain that God was saying to me, '...establish a permanent ministry there.' But just how was I to do this? Gradually, over some years of prayer, negotiations, discussion and diocesan changes, it happened. By 1987, the church had its own distinct budget. A new parsonage was built. The church building had been re-ordered to seat a growing congregation, which trebled in size. St. Martin's became an independent parish in 1993. The change to financial independence at St. Martin's was important. It enabled us to begin tithing our church income for outward giving. The church had been over-dependent on jumble sales. In the early days, Fran and I often came home to discover that a bag of jumble had been left on the doorstep. Hardly the right image for a church proclaiming the Gospel! We had stopped all this, making the point strongly that our giving should be tithed. Giving increased and we were able to assist a Romanian pastor in building a church and ministry team. We saw the Lord's power at work in so many ways. There were conversions, and miracles of healing. I had seen God change my life, and I was privileged to see Him change the lives of others. But first I had had to learn to give Him the glory!

The Lord is gracious—we know that—but His grace is beyond our comprehension. He had taken me, a secular Jew from a working class background in North London, a man of no proven academic ability, a man with no spiritual understanding at all. He had placed me in the right place at the right time, and had given me all the gifts I needed to do what He wanted of me. He had assured me that His love for me was full of forgiveness. No matter how bad I had been, He accepted me. No matter how disobedient I had been, He welcomed me. Such love, O Jesus, such love! He had taught me that my place in the Kingdom is guaranteed, not because of my abilities, thankfully, for I do not have many, but because of His abounding grace at work in me.

I learnt much during my time at St. Martin's, but the Lord had another major change in store for me, which involved both new self-understanding and a new area of work. At Bookham, we had had one or two embarrassing experiences regarding my Jewishness, and I had vowed that I would never speak of it again. After all, I was a Christian, not a Jew, and in any event it was not possible to be both a Jew and a Christian. That is what I sincerely believed then; but, again, God had plans to show me the error of my ways.

Visiting Israel had never been on my agenda. I had no interest in what was going on in that country. If pressed, I think I would have said that I was anti-Zionist; that the establishment of the State of Israel in 1948 was definitely not in accordance with the will of God. My sister had a holiday in Israel in 1988, and began to put some pressure on me to go. I developed a response, 'I will not go to Israel, until Jerusalem lives up to her name, and is the city of peace.' That, I thought, would keep me from going.

Then Fran got the feeling that I should go: and when she received a flyer from the Bethany Fellowship, about a four week study tour to Israel for ministers in October 1990, she said that she thought I *should* go. 'No', I said, 'Not until Jerusalem ....'

Fran is a dutiful wife, and she simply smiled and said something like, 'As you wish', but two weeks later I received a letter from the Bethany Fellowship, expressing their delight that I had shown an interest in their forthcoming four week study tour of Israel!

After some 'discussion', Fran and I decided to 'lay a fleece' before the Lord: If the diocese (a) agreed to let me have a four week mini sabbatical; and, (b) agreed to pay for the trip, I should take that as a sign that I should go. I really thought that I was on safe ground. Imagine then my utter astonishment, when I was summoned for an interview with the Director of in-service training. He told me that he and the bishop had discussed my case already. They were both convinced that it would be a good thing for me to go, and gave me a cheque for the full cost of the tour plus a sum for spending money.

So to Israel I went! And then began the most significant period of my life to date. The tour was planned for two months after Saddam Hussein had invaded Kuwait, when the whole Middle East was in a new dimension of tension. Consequently, many tour groups had cancelled. Indeed, within my own group, most of the clergy who had booked had cancelled too. Thus the group was made up primarily of Colin Urquhart's staff members from the Hyde. To begin with, it was a group I did not really want to be part of, and we were in a country which I did not particularly want be in. My old self, the rebellious self, was very much to the fore.

On the fourth day of the tour, we arrived in Jerusalem. After dinner, we went to the Western Wall. The guide explained to us the significance of the Wall. Then, as he spoke, something began to stir in me. That 'something' became insistent when he then explained the circumstances behind a massacre which had taken place on the Temple Mount just ten days earlier, when the Israeli Defence Forces had shot and killed twenty one Arabs, who had been throwing stones on Jewish worshippers below. The 'something' snapped, when the guide then told me that the group of worshippers had all been Russian immigrants, giving thanks for their Aliyah (homecoming) and that all of them were COHANIM (Cohens).

I knew that I had to pray at the Wall. So I went forward, collecting a cardboard KIPPAH as I went, and stood at the Wall, and berated God: just as Tevye the milkman does in 'Fiddler On The Roof'.

'Why have you brought me here, to a country I did not want to visit, with a group I don't want to be part of? Why have you taken me away from family, home and ministry for a four week period against my will?' Finally, spent and confused, I gave the Lord a chance to get a word in, and He did! 'Neil, you are a Jew first.'

He said it again. I usually need to hear things two or three times before they sink in. 'Neil, you are a Jew first.'

The next three and a half weeks were wonderful. I knew then that being in Israel was just like a homecoming for me. This is where I belong; this is where all my history comes from and is going to; this is my national homeland. I belong here. Coming back to England was dreadful; I did not want to leave Israel, I had found my real and deepest self here, and I could not bear the thought of leaving it behind—of course I didn't. It felt so painful as we taxied away to the take off runway at Ben Gurion Airport.

Fran's first words to me when she met me at Heathrow, were 'You want to go back, don't you.' Of course I did, how could I not, the call was from the deepest part of my being, deep calling to deep, and I knew that I could not ignore or resist it.

Eighteen months later, we all went as a family, and had three wonderful weeks, holidaying in the land of my birthright, and we experienced a deep sense of 'this is the start of something quite amazing.'

In 1995 I took a full sabbatical, and went to Israel to write a book of my testimony[1], and while I was there three especially significant things happened. First, I became convinced that I was soon to leave the parish in Camberley, and move on to a new work. I prayed for guidance about this, but seemed to receive none. All I knew was that I was not missing the church in Camberley, as I normally did when away even for a day or two. Second, I experienced Messianic worship. I visited as many of the Messianic congregations as I could while in Israel, and actually stayed on a Messianic Moshav for the full time I was there. Third, my father died: I had to come home for his funeral a week earlier than I had planned. I wrestled with thoughts which a rabbi expressed concerning heaven.

I resolved to find out as much as I could about the Jewish religion, and how it differed from Christianity. So began a new phase of studying this subject. At the end of that period of reflection and study, I had to conclude that not only is it possible for me as a Jew to be a Christian, but this is indeed the *completion* of my Jewishness. To put that round the other way, not only is it possible for me as a Christian to hold on to my Jewishness, it fulfilled my Christianity in a way that was God's plan for me.

Now I understood the words of Jesus when he said that he had not come to abolish the Law but to fulfil it. Now I understood how the Church and synagogue had become separated. Now I understood the pain within the Jewish community when the name of Jesus Christ is used. Now I understood so much of the shame and confusion that had marked the church in her relationship with the Jewish People for two thousand years. Now I understood—and I burned with a passion to do something about it.

It was a source of immense joy therefore to receive an invitation to apply for a position with the Church's Ministry Among Jewish People. I had known of CMJ for a couple of years, had been to St. Alban's to meet some of the staff there, and the General Director had come to preach at our church in Camberley. So it was that in January 1996 I left parish ministry and joined CMJ as Regional Adviser for the South East of England. Despite all the learning I had been doing over the past four years, I was aware that what I knew was hopelessly inadequate. A steep learning curve lay ahead of me. In rock-climbing terms I saw it as an overhang! But the Lord has equipped, and where He saw gaps in my knowledge He led me to the right books, and the right people.

With CMJ I have been an itinerant preacher and teacher, and have discovered a degree of fulfilment that I thought was impossible. The period in Church of England parish ministry was special, but working in CMJ turned out to be *extra* special. It continues to be a source of astonishment to me that so many Christian people are unaware of the Jewish-ness of Jesus, or even of how important it is that he was a Jew. The Church has taught for so long that God has finished with the Jewish people, and that the Church is now the Israel of God. He has shown me that this is simply not the case. If it were, He would not be a covenant-keeping God, and this is one of the characteristics that we love so much about Him. It means that He can be trusted to keep His word. If He had broken His word to Israel, then He would have been just as likely to break His word to the Church, and that is unthinkable!

No, He has kept His promises to Israel. He still regards them as the apple of His eye. He is still committed to protect them and love them, in order that they may fulfil their obligation to Him to be a nation of priests, and to bring the whole world into the covenant relationship with Him, which is theirs along with all believers in Jesus, through the promises to Abraham, Isaac and Jacob.

This same God is also the one who is able to do far more abundantly than all we can ask or imagine—and who could ever have imagined at the beginning of my journey that I would end up with what I consider to be the best job in the world!

In the Spring of 1999, the position of Rector of Christ Church Jerusalem became vacant. Being a man of little humility, I thought, 'I could do that!' So I applied for the post, not really daring to believe that I would even be short-listed, let alone offered the job. The Lord is so gracious—He wanted me in that post, and He paved the way: there were many prophecies from friends that I was the one meant for the post.

We heard at the interview that the congregation at Christ Church were spending the day of the interview in prayer and fasting, and that they had been led to pray for 'a David'. Neither Fran nor I understood at the time what that meant, but later we pondered, and the pieces began to fall together.

One of the interviewing panel had begun to weep as soon as I started to answer one of the questions. Quite nonplussed, I decided to ignore this for the moment but to seek a time to ask her about it later. When I did ask she told me that, as I began to speak, the Lord whispered to her, 'He is the man.' When Samuel went to Jesse's house to anoint the successor to King Saul, and after all the sons had been paraded before the prophet, he asked, 'is there any other?' Jesse called David in from the fields where he had been tending the family flocks. As he approached Samuel, the Lord said to him, 'Rise and anoint him, he is the one.' (1Samuel 16:12b)

Thus you find me now in the Old City of Jerusalem, as rector of the only Anglican Church within its walls; rector of the oldest protestant church in the Middle East. What an amazing and gracious God we serve, to endow me, entrust me, privilege me with such an awesome task. In His strength, we can do all things, and I pray that so we shall.

As I look back over the thirty years since I met Father Ken, I can see how the Lord has guided me, led me, and cajoled me. I see so clearly now the pattern, the strands of the tapestry. I see so clearly the route by which He has brought me from being a totally unbelieving, secular Jew, to ordination into Christian ministry, into the fullness of the Baptism of the Holy Spirit; and now into the realisation that being—as I put it—a 'born-again Jew', I am best equipped to serve Him. My whole life is pointing to the here and now, to this ministry, to this moment in my life when I can share, with whoever will listen, His plans for the world. I see through the eyes of a Jewish believer, who is an Anglican priest (there are not many of us). Above all, I now understand that the ministry to which I am called is wider than one parish, wider than the vital task of bringing people into salvation, wider even than pastoring and shepherding them into the fullness of the Spirit. The ministry with which I have been entrusted is also a ministry of reconciliation: to reconcile Christian people to the roots of our faith, and to reconcile Jewish people to their Messiah. For this ministry, I am grateful to God, and dependent on Him for a daily anointing to fulfil it to His glory.

[1] *My Road Home* (Terra Nova, 1996)

Born of the Spirit

MICHAEL BENNETT

Vicar of Llansantffraid-ym-Mechain,
Rector of Llanfechain, Powys, and
Vice-Chairman of Anglican Renewal Ministries, Wales

I was trained for the ministry at King's College London in the early sixties. The 'in-word' in those days seemed to be 'de-mythologise'. The academic training was superb, but the message was that modern man could not make sense of such doctrines as the virgin birth or the resurrection. They had to be re-interpreted. It was the day of Thomas Altizer and *The Gospel of Christian Atheism*, Harvey Cox and *The Secular City* and John Robinson and *Honest to God*. We were discouraged from talking about the supernatural. Many began to question what the rôle of the Church really was.

One day, a certain professor was happily de-mythologising the resurrection. In the discussion which followed, a student asked, 'That's all very well, but what would you say at a funeral?' The professor replied that he had not officiated at a funeral for twenty five years. I am afraid that I switched off after that. His rhetoric may have seemed fine in the rarefied atmosphere of a university college, but in a few months' time I would be out in a parish, where people asked questions; and what answers would I give?

In 1967 I began my title curacy in the parish of Chester-le-Street, in the Durham diocese. My experiences there were to show how damaging so-called modern theology can be. Man needs spiritual food. If he is not nourished by the Christian Church, he will turn to other things. I believe that the rise of interest in the occult and Eastern religion is related to scepticism in the Church, flowing from rationalism. De-mythologising was a result. As G. K. Chesterton said, 'When people give up the Christian faith, they don't believe in nothing, they believe in anything.'

It was not long after I had been ordained that I discovered people who had had spiritual experiences. They told me about things that had happened which we might call psychic experiences, and of how they had gone to spiritualists because the clergy could not help them.

My wife and I had a lovely neighbour who was a spiritualist. I had long talks with her, and she persuaded me to attend a home circle. We sang hymns and prayed. People received 'messages' —it all seemed very spiritual and I do not doubt the sincerity and honesty of those who attended. I was convinced for a time, but things began to happen to me. I lost my desire to read God's Word. I began to be critical of the Church. The rector and the other curate began to be concerned about what I was preaching. One day I went into the parish church and picked up a prayer book, throwing it from one side of the church to the other. I began to read the spiritualist newspaper *Psychic News* and to write to Harry Edwards at his 'healing sanctuary'. I went to see him when he visited Newcastle, taking a girl from the youth club with me.

I was going away from Jesus, and the deceiver was at work within me. However, God is good. One day I had to go and see the Bishop of Jarrow, Alex Hamilton, who had oversight of the newly ordained in the Durham diocese. I told him that I felt I needed guidance in the psychic realm, and that there should be something for clergy, where these matters could be discussed. I had already raised the subject at a clergy school some months earlier, with the Bishop of Durham, Ian Ramsey. He was sympathetic. But afterwards, two of my contemporaries from college, who had been ordained with me, rebuked me. 'How could you, with your King's training, bring up the subject of "ghosts" with the bishop?' I was not supposed to believe in the supernatural any more! Yet I knew that there was a spiritual realm, which the Church must acknowledge if it were not to lose people, often to spiritualists and other cults.

In the event, a number of groups were set up in the diocese, for post-ordination training for clergy of all ages. One group was to deal with problems raised by psychical phenomena. I put my name down for this group, which was led by Peter Brett, then a chaplain at the University of Durham, later a residentiary canon of Canterbury Cathedral. At last I began to get a Christian perspective, as we studied such subjects as ley-lines, poltergeists, exorcism, witchcraft, and so on. I began to see that here was a challenging but dangerous realm, in which one must rely on Jesus every step of the way. Those who wandered into it without

Christ were easy prey for the devices of Satan, who was a fallen angel. Angels and demons do exist, after all! I was reminded that in C. S. Lewis' book *The Screwtape Letters*, Screwtape encourages Wormwood to make people think that devils do not exist. I thought of so many theological lectures I had heard. There was one by a bishop who said that if we believe in a devil we face the problem 'who made the devil?' The answer according to the Bible, of course, is that God made the devil, but he and some of the angels rebelled against God. The devil was thrown down from heaven. Jesus told his disciples that he witnessed it (Luke 10:18). The Book of Job portrays Satan not as all-powerful, but rather like a dog on a lead. He can only do what God allows him to do.

While at Chester-le-Street, I became acquainted with the Church's healing ministry, through the Guild of Health and other people who had experience in this area. Peter Brett suggested it would be good for members of the diocesan group to attend a national conference of the exorcism study group. One of the organisers was John Richards, then a curate at All Saints, Bournemouth—the church in which I had been married, a few years prior to this. My mother-in-law told me about John's healing ministry. God was working out His purposes.

I moved from Chester-le-Street to a second curacy at All Saints, Portland, Dorset, in the Diocese of Salisbury. Then, in 1972, I attended for the first time an exorcism study group conference at Queen's College, Birmingham. Participants came from many denominations, ranging from Roman Catholic to Pentecostal; and some came from overseas.

Here I felt a tremendous oneness with all these Christians who were united in knowing the victory of Jesus over the power of the enemy. It was here that I met Michael and Jeanne Harper, and other pioneers of renewal. For the first time I heard tongues. Of course I had heard about tongues before, but had thought Anglicans did not do that sort of thing! Yet the Harpers seemed sensible people. There was no doubt they had 'something', but it was not yet for me. A year later, I was back for the conference again. It was good to see Professor Eric Mascall from King's College. Most people at the college had thought his theology out of date, yet he had an understanding of the spiritual realms that more theologians could do with.

Yet over my life hung a long shadow. It was September 1973. In June our second son Christopher had been born. We had noticed quite early that things were not right. In fact he was blind, and there was the possibility of other handicaps. He was suffering from a condition known as Rhyger's Syndrome. To say that my wife and I were devastated was an understatement. I began to feel that here was a punishment from God for my involvement in spiritualism. All my failings as a priest began to haunt me. Satan is the great accuser, and he was sticking the knife in.

I arrived in Birmingham for the conference with a heavy heart, yet looking for the uplift I had felt the year before. On the second day of the conference, I was with two other people in conversation with a sweet Methodist lady. She talked about the blessings of baptism in the Holy Spirit. We tended to be rather critical, suggesting that it might just be emotion. It was fine for others, but not for me—yet I needed God to ease the pain in my heart as I thought of Christopher, and my wife Sheila, so brave but so utterly devastated.

One of the speakers at the conference was Dennis Peterson, then Vicar of St. Jude's, Brixton. Whereas at the conference we saw bishops with silver crosses and fine suits, Dennis often wore a leather jacket with badges saying 'Jesus loves you'. He had one of the toughest parishes in the country, yet he radiated happiness. I had to talk to him. How God seems to have a sense of humour! I was a King's man; Dennis was from Oak Hill Theological College, at the other end of the spectrum. How we used to despise those 'holy Joes' from that evangelical 'ghetto' at Southgate, who neither drank nor smoked, and talked about 'being saved'. (They did in the 1960s.) However, I knew Dennis could help me, so I asked if we could have a talk. He invited me to his room after lunch. I poured it all out: my doubts, my fears, my involvement with spiritualism. When I had finished, Dennis simply said, 'Well, brother, all we can do is to take it to the Lord.'

I knelt on the floor and confessed my sins, renouncing my involvement with spiritualism. Dennis prayed, laying his hands on my head. I began to breathe heavily. I could feel something coming out of my stomach; it seemed to come right up through my throat and out of my mouth. I was coughing. There was a foul smell, and Dennis was saying, 'Come out, you foul thing, in the name of Jesus.' I had been delivered. An evil spirit had been cast out. I began to feel a great peace. Then I began to say, 'Christopher will see; Christopher will see.' Was I going mad? No: God was giving me a prophecy. Dennis had been praying in tongues for some of the time, and now he asked me whether I had received the gift. I told him that I had not, but that I was overjoyed

90

for all that the Lord had done, and that in fact I had never asked for or desired the gift of tongues. Now I felt wonderful: all my fears and doubts seemed to have gone. But the Lord had not yet finished His work in me.

It was the evening and I was in bed, thanking the Lord for the blessings of the day. Suddenly, I began to pray in a strange language, which flowed out of my mouth for over an hour. I had received the gift of tongues. Next day I told Dennis, and the dear Methodist lady, who was delighted to hear of what had happened.

I returned to Portland, full of what the Lord had done. Sheila could see what a change there was in me, but found it hard to accept. In November, Christopher went into the Weymouth Eye Infirmary. He was under the care of Giles Romanes, a brilliant eye surgeon, who drove traction engines for a hobby. A cautious man, he did not promise that he could do anything for someone so young, but he was willing to try a corneal graft. Christopher was one of the youngest patients on which he had performed this operation. When he saw Christopher after the operation, he was quite excited over the results. As the months passed, it was obvious that Christopher could see. The prophecy had been fulfilled.

Our problem now was how to relate what I had experienced to the life of a traditional Anglican parish. I recounted some of my experiences to my rector, the late Howard Bell, whose father Edgar Bell had exercised a healing ministry. Howard was a good friend to me and he happened to have a letter from a former church youth group member. She had moved to Luton and was attending a church where strange things were taking place. It was St. Hugh's, Lewsey, and the vicar had recently had a book published. It was entitled *When the Spirit Comes*, and its author was Colin Urquhart. I read the book, and what a revelation it was—and Colin was a Kingsman. Another Kingsman, David Stoter, a contemporary of mine, was mentioned in the book as being his curate. I will always remember the evening I visited St. Hugh's. The church was packed for the service, which began at 6.30 p.m. and lasted for over two and a half hours. I was sorry when it ended. The girl from our youth group was in the congregation, and I can recall her leaping over the pews to give my wife and myself a big hug.

In those early days of renewal in the Holy Spirit, Sheila and I were greatly helped by Reg East and the community at Whatcombe House, near Blandford. I had been renewed but Sheila was still finding it hard to accept, so we went to a family week, taking our sons Richard and Christopher with us. Sheila was greatly helped by the ministry and we went there several times as a family. On one occasion, Christopher was with my wife in a discussion group at one of Whatcombe's family weeks. There was a lady in the group who complained rather bitterly about her misfortunes until Christopher began to sing a song he had recently learnt. It was called 'Jesus loves Kristi'. He sang the line, 'Jesus loves everyone, yes he does.' Hearing him sing, the lady burst into tears. A very nice nun who was also in the group said to me, 'Christopher has been ministering to us.' As the Scripture says, 'From the lips of children and infants you have ordained praise' (Matt 21:16).

At Whatcombe on another occasion, I was talking to a young housewife from Canford Magna Parish. We found that we had something in common, having both been to school in Darlington. As she spoke, I had the feeling that she was not well. The following morning, she and I were in the same discussion group, meeting in the chapel. Our group leader asked us all to pray in turn. When it was her turn, she thanked the Lord that she felt better than she had the night before. I knew then that I had to pray with her. I felt very reticent. Although I had only met her the night before, the Lord was prompting me. The group meeting ended and people began to move out of the chapel. I went to her as she got up to leave and, with a great feeling of embarrassment, told her that I believed the Lord wanted me to pray with her. To my great relief she agreed, and I asked her to kneel at the altar rail. I laid hands on her and, not really knowing what to say, rather nervously prayed: 'Lord, we come before you, asking healing for Wanda.' Then I felt a great sense of the Lord's power and prayed with authority in the Name of Jesus, and also prayed in tongues.

At lunchtime, Wanda told me how much better she felt. A few days later she wrote to me, saying that she was completely healed. Some weeks later I visited Wanda and her husband David. He told me what a difference it had made to their lives when Wanda came back from Whatcombe completely healed. He said to me it was because I had obeyed the Lord. I admitted that I had not really wanted to, but the Lord had overcome my reticence.

I was to have a number of happy visits to Canford Magna in the next few years, to see a parish in the midst of a tremendous renewal, under the then vicar, John Collins, and his curate Brian Nicholson. John Richards was also nearby as a chaplain at Canford School.

In 1974 I became Vicar of St. John the Baptist, Portland. It was a traditional parish and I succeeded a much-loved and respected priest who had shown me much kindness during my time in the neighbouring parish of All Saints. Renewal brings great blessings, but it can also bring much pain. At St. John's I experienced both. There was resistance to change, which was to be expected. Someone who was not a church member, but came to me late one night for help as he was on the verge of suicide, said as he talked to me through the early hours, 'People say you are a revolutionary.' As he left, he said to me, 'You have saved a life tonight.' I saw that I must be a priest to all the people. That is what the Church of England claims to be—the church for all the people. In fact, so often its way of worship is too narrow. Often it rejects those who want to be free of the ritual and liturgical straitjacket. I prayed for renewal. A prayer group was formed, which co-incided with a time of crisis in the parish when there was a marriage break-up involving two prominent members of the congregation.

Changes came in the Parish Communion, which became less formal, and eventually a music group, formed from the young people's group, became a regular feature. Younger people began to appear more in the church, and I tried to persuade people of all ages that God wanted to bless them.

Several remarkable things happened in my time in Dorset. I attended a conference at Whatcombe on the ministry of deliverance. A woman at the conference was delivered from a past in Satanism. When she was prayed for, I was kneeling on one side of her. When it came to the moment of deliverance, the strength she had was amazing. I was being pushed sideways. She was held the other side by a member of the community, while a clergyman who is well-known in the ministry of deliverance laid hands on her. Gradually she grew calmer and said, 'They've gone' —words straight out of Scripture. Remember the story of Jesus and the Gadarene demoniac (St. Mark, Chapter 5). The important point here is that there was prayer back-up, with other people being present.

Now for a cautionary tale. In the early years of my ministry, in a certain parish (I will not say which; I was sometimes asked by other clergy to see their parishioners), I counselled a person who had been involved in satanism as a child. Many terrible things were done to this person, and I knew that deliverance was necessary. One day I decided to pray for deliverance, as the person was in bed, unwell. I should not have attempted this alone, but Jesus has the victory. I began to pray and, although the person was very weak, they went into a trance, sat bolt upright in bed, and hands came around my throat. A gravelly voice came out of the person, with these words, 'Who do you think you are, I'll teach you not to meddle.'

I was being strangled, but I said, 'I claim the precious blood of Jesus; I bind you, Satan. Get out.' Gradually, the grip was released and the person fell back on the bed. When they awoke and saw my rather shaken expression, I was asked to explain what had happened. I simply said that we had a visitor but he had gone. The person was delivered, but this is a dangerous ministry which should not be undertaken alone. Jesus sent out the seventy-two in pairs. (See Luke, Chapter 10).

Many healings took place during my time at St. John's. We had a prayer, praise and healing meeting at 8 p.m. on Sundays, after Evensong. There was not a large congregation, but we often heard tongues, interpretation and prophecy.

Later in my ministry, elsewhere, a most dramatic healing occurred in someone's home. I was praying with someone who was very ill. They stopped breathing. I was halfway out of the room to telephone doctor and relatives when I felt the Lord telling me to return. I went back to the bed and breathed on the person, who revived. For about a week that person was disappointed. I was told that they had met Jesus and had a vision of heaven. Jesus told the person that they were coming back to help me. So that person felt a sense of rejection for a while as they did not want to return to a life of pain. Jesus raises the dead today.

It was good to see a church in renewal, but I felt the Lord was telling me to leave St. John's. I still do not know the reason why. I went for seven years to two rural parishes in the West Midlands. After I left Portland, St. John's returned to a more traditional churchmanship. Some people went to other churches. Others, who could not easily accept renewal, came back. It is not for me to judge what happened, though it caused me pain; but it is God's church, not ours, and He knows best. He sees the whole picture; we only see a small portion. Renewal carried on in Portland: first at the Naval Church, then at All Saints. It is well to read Paul's epistles as they show us that in the life of the early church there was much blessing, but pain too.

I will not say much about the two rural parishes. They contain many fine people, some of whom have come into renewal. I found great joy in having fellowship with the local Methodists, Bridgenorth Baptist

Church and St. Pius Roman Catholic Church, Kidderminster, where I was privileged to minister with their priest, Father Stephen Squires and his people, at their healing masses. To pray with people, many of whom 'went out in the Spirit' in a Roman Catholic setting was marvellous.

Many years ago, while at Portland, I attended one of the conferences of the Fountain Trust. At the end of the day, people would gather in rooms to pray. I was in a group where they prayed and people fell to the floor. That was *not* going to happen to me.... However, I was prayed with and out I went. It was wonderful. I was then asked if I would pray with someone. No way would anyone fall down if I prayed with them.... I laid hands on a man and down he went! One of the group, a Baptist deacon, told me that this was a sign that the Lord would use me in the healing ministry.

In my West Midlands parishes, I encouraged people to see that there is more, and not to be content with traditional Anglicanism. One person complained of having 'Holy Spirit indigestion' because of my sermons referring to God's work. When Jesus went to Nazareth, he could not do much because of their unbelief. They also tried to throw him over the cliff. I was not thrown over a cliff, but a meeting was held one night, to discuss whether I could be removed from the parish. One of the assistant clergy was left to tell me what had taken place. I make no apology for the fact that I believe one hundred per cent in the virgin birth, the resurrection and second coming of Christ. I believe that Christian ministers have the authority to cast out demons, heal the sick and raise the dead, and I have experienced all three.

Through the difficult time when letters were written, for and against me, I was very aware of the love and prayers of many in the parish. I was greatly encouraged by Anglican Renewal Ministry conferences. It is wonderful to see what God is doing in His church. For several years I took people from the parish to Swanwick for the September annual national conference. One year, when I was going through a difficult time of opposition, I took with me to the conference a dear person who has known pain and sorrow in her life. During one session we were encouraged to pray for one another. I asked her to pray with me. She was not sure what to say, but I knew that God would give her the right words, as He had given me the right words when praying with Wanda, many years before. She laid her hands on my head and the words came out. I broke down and wept; all the pain and rejection came out, and I could feel the love of Christ bringing healing and strength.

The ways of worship changed little in the parish churches where I was then ministering. It was a time of many blessings for individuals. It was also a time of judgement and it is significant that, since my successor has arrived, those who opposed me no longer worship in the parish. God will never bless rebellion, as it is the devil's tool to disunite the church. Satan does not worry about dead churches. They are no threat to his kingdom. But when fellowships and individuals move in the Spirit of God, one can expect opposition from the prince of darkness.

There are people in my former parishes who are doing beautiful things in the power of the Lord and joining together with other parishes and churches receiving blessings.

Many people were surprised that I should leave an attractive area, a new luxurious vicarage with its views of the Severn Valley and Clee Hills, to go into the Prison Service. One person said to me, 'How can you mix with murderers and rapists?' The answer to that is that Jesus mixed with them. I began my work with young offenders at Glen Parva, one of the largest establishments of its kind. Having not been involved in ministry to prisoners since my time in Portland, I had not thought that I would be led by the Lord to enter such work full-time.

My time in the Prison Service was to be one of strengthening, and learning new skills. A whole new world opened up. I have seen harshness, cynicism and fear, but also beauty and peace, as God has touched troubled lives. Prisoners are very honest about themselves. They readily welcome the chaplain to pray with them. They show a willingness to hear the gospel which people in churches do not always show. They ask direct questions—about the Bible, about Christian faith. God does wonderful things in prison and, although some do re-offend and return, others go out and become powerful witnesses for Jesus, seeking to bring to Christ other young people embarking on a life of crime.

So often it is not the prisoners who cause problems for chaplains, but a system which ensnares officer, governors and members of other disciplines as well; a system which is becoming increasingly bureaucratic and centred on accounts rather than people.

Just before I started work at Glen Parva, my father died, following a long illness. I gave the address at his funeral and I felt the love and power of Jesus. It was a great joy to proclaim to family and friends that Jesus lives, as do his faithful people who have died. After the service, an aunt said to me that she could not understand how I had been able to give the address at my own father's funeral. She said, 'I suppose it's your training.' She meant my theological training but, unlike the professor so many years before, I knew what to say for my training has come from the Holy Spirit.

The time spent in the Prison Service proved to be another turning point in my life. I had been just too young to be called up for National Service, but had always wished that I had been able to serve in a disciplined environment. A full time chaplain in the Prison Service is paid by the Home Office and classified a civil servant. So I now had a secular employer, whose practice was to require staff reports on its employees. Some have suggested that churches should do this for the clergy. It might be helpful. For the first time, I had to read of how others saw me—and the comments were not always flattering! But when an employee thinks them to be unfair, he can bring the matter to the attention of a union, which chaplains are invited to join. On the whole, the experience of being in a setting which was quite different from parish life was a beneficial one for me. It was indeed disciplined, and one was always racing against the clock. A typical working weekday began at 7.30 a.m. and ended at 8.30 p.m., though unlike many parochial clergy one had two days off per week, and generous leave. Chaplaincy work is ecumenical, so there were other denominations to work with, as well as lay assistants, whose work helped inmates on release. Denominational labels were far less significant than outside prison. Interviewing new arrivals, I was able to stress that whether or not they had a religion, the chaplain could be seen as a friend, and that one of their rights while in custody was to see the chaplain at any time. I felt it was a real problem that fifteen and twenty year olds were remanded together. Some of the twenty year olds could be on their third or fourth visit to us and what the fifteen year olds did not know when they arrived they knew when they left. A good number of inmates chose to attend the (voluntary) chapel services. That many of the young people put themselves down as 'no religion' was not because they had made a decision against faith, but that they knew nothing of any church—few had had contact with organized religion of any sort. Many asked for Bibles to read in their cells. The chaplaincy stocked books written by ex-convicts and by chaplains, about people coming to know Christ, and these publications were popular because they started where the prisoners were. Equally popular were visits to the chapel by former inmates who had become Christians. It has to be said that renewal in the Holy Spirit can be a problem for any chaplain in a secular organization. One clerical colleague over me (whom I greatly respected) was nonetheless deeply suspicious of renewal. He expected me to be exuberant, not perhaps realizing that meditation is as much part of renewal as being 'happy-clappy'.

Despite the frustrations of the work, there was great joy in seeing so many of the young inmates come to know the Lord. Whatever people have done, they are human beings who need to know that they are loved. They often have strange relationships. Some had lived with women older than themselves with children by other partners. Some had witnessed cruelty and rejection in their families, and found it hard to love and respect others. All were damaged people. What prison should try to do is to repair the damage. Just locking people up is not enough.

Some months before I decided to resign from the Prison Service, a priest came to Glen Parva, to gain experience of the work. He had worked as a Church Army Captain in the Wrexham Team Ministry. He asked me whether I had ever worked in the Church in Wales. Then the post of Team Vicar of Wrexham was advertised. I had rather rashly prayed that I would accept the first parish that offered me a job! So it was that I moved to St. Mark's, which serves the largest housing estate in North Wales. It could be rough at times. I could not say no to the Lord: I had promised. This was it. In the new parish, we found there were many social problems—vandalism, unemployment, under-age drinking. At St. Mark's I did not know where to start, but the Lord impressed upon me that there should be a prayer group and a healing ministry. We began a formal laying-on-of-hands at a monthly eucharist, and a monthly gospel praise service, at which ministry is available. I looked for a renewal prayer group in Wrexham, and found it at the Roman Catholic Cathedral. Moving on to Wales, I felt that I should become acquainted with Anglican Renewal Ministries (Wales). So I found myself at the *Flames of Fire* conference at Cefn Lea in 1995. In that year the Lord gave the vision to move the event to a larger venue— the Royal Welsh Showground, Builth Wells. A family conference on the lines of *New Wine*, *Flames of Fire* has been blessed with growth, year by year.

In 1996 I was elected to serve as Vice-Chairman of ARM (Wales) and it is wonderful to see the way God is blessing so many people in Wales, through ministry in the Holy Spirit. Praise services with Barry Kissell were held in cathedrals around the principality in 1997, and our diocese of St. Asaph now has a group to promote charismatic renewal. In Wrexham, as elsewhere, we see exciting developments as Alpha courses spring up. The loyal congregation at St. Mark's continues to plant seeds that will come to fruition.

The Lord is still opening new horizons for me, with a move to my new parishes. He continues to change me, as He goes on changing the lives of all who are open to the work of His Spirit. My desire is to grow closer to Him as a 'servant of the Living God' —the God who goes on changing us and drawing us to Himself, throughout our lives.

Waves of the Spirit

NICOLAS LEIGH-HUNT

Team Rector of the Wexcombe Team Ministry in Wiltshire

I was thirty five when I met with Christ—quite a late stage—so my Christian life has been really quite a short period, during which I have been conscious of the Lord's hand upon me. Sometimes, of course, I have become aware of His guidance only with the aid of hindsight. The blessings and pains have followed so hard upon each other that I have long ceased trying to be too analytical about what God's purposes might be.

It would be stretching it to say that I had a Christian upbringing. But as a child I had a powerful input of middle class ethic and values, which many would take to be the same thing and, in early days, I was regularly taken to a 'children's service'. In a somewhat rebellious youth, one of my few redeeming features was that I was musical. That found expression as a chorister at the Chapel Royal, Hampton Court Palace; and then I won a choral scholarship to New College, Oxford.

So as a young person I was well-versed in formal religion. At fourteen I was confirmed: and although I remember little of the preparation for that, I had certainly led myself to believe this was to be the point of 'spiritual arrival'. A few months beyond the event therefore, unsurprisingly, I felt fairly flat, and wondered what else there was to know about God. Strangely, though, there was a strand deep within me which would not let go of the idea that God should have some real significance in my life. Feelings, and even the more churchy 'spirituality' were never on any religious agenda, and I do not recall the concept of 'relationship' with God ever getting an airing.

It is easy to sound critical of course, but the choral tradition which formed so much of my early years was a hard taskmaster, with specific objectives of very high standards, only achieved with strict disciplines and timetables. The public school tradition of my teenage years has a pretty universalistic culture, wary of making its historic parental base uneasy with anything too strident and, certainly where we were located (north of London), there was no wish to alienate the very considerable input from Jewish families and those of other religious backgrounds from around the world.

That, in a nutshell, brings me to adulthood. In the cut and thrust of forging a career in business, marriage at a fairly early stage, mortgages and children, I became, like my father, a 'three times a year' church attender, and 'God', invoked other than in church, or at least with the right tones of crematorium music in the background, was an embarrassment to me. I was far too busy doing other things anyway for Him to be likely to get much of a mention.

This spiritually 'fallow' period for me came to an end when our second child, Naomi, was born. With due respect for tradition, we applied to the local parish church for her to be baptised. Up to this point we had been perfunctory attenders. There was a new vicar who seemed to have a measure of drive and enthusiasm, and in the process we found ourselves drawn in—at least to a Sunday morning routine which was socially agreeable and did not seem to demand anything. We were then posted to Italy.

This was our second spell outside the UK, so we picked up the traces of expatriate living quickly, and in Milan the English-speaking church was an obvious focus. My experience of church quickly drew me on to the church council and I was appointed a churchwarden.

The mobility of population in the expatriate community was high. It was after a year or so we started to notice those around us, and I became aware that there were two families—very similar to ourselves in many ways, with small children—who were different. It was not something I could put my finger on, and of course for some time was a thing of which I was aware but not aware—a quality of confidence, authority, assurance about who they were and where they were going which, despite my international manager's exterior, I did not have. They also disconcertingly talked of Jesus as if he were in the room next door.

By the time this was beginning to eat at me, we were posted back to the UK again. We recovered our home and picked up the traces of English community life, including, of course, the church. I was 'scooped up' by the institution and within a short time, surprise, surprise, I was elected into office as a churchwarden again. Yet even at an early stage of the mixture of euphoria and hard work that being in demand placed on me, I was aware (because I recognised it more quickly this time) that there was a handful of people here too who were—different. A long year followed before the penny dropped——a long story in itself—when I was asked out of the blue, or so it seemed at the time (though God's timing is impeccable), 'Have you ever committed your life to Christ?'

In a moment the world stood still, but in that moment I realised that was the key question, and in a lifetime in the Church of England, no-one had ever asked it of me before. I made that commitment at last!

It was about six months after this breakthrough that I first learned something of the Holy Spirit. The 'Holy Ghost', yes, I had heard of; he was mentioned once a year on Whitsunday, without any serious explanation of the extraordinary goings-on in Acts 2, and we were customarily given a vague conclusion that he was supposed to help us with our prayer life. The first 'glow' of becoming a Christian had by this stage worn off, and sometimes I was not sure whether I was much better off than before I had made that step of faith towards Jesus.

'Have you been baptised in the Spirit?' a lady of the church who had taken me under her wing demanded of me.

'Er, um, er...' I started to respond.

'Then you haven't!' she said, and insisted on praying for me within the week. The effect was not dramatic, and I got up from kneeling on the floor one evening, consciously thinking that I did not feel any different. But I knew something in me had changed, and from that day I knew I was beginning to see things from God's perspective rather than just my own. The focus, at least initially, seemed more than anything else on the flaws and inconsistencies in my own character and lifestyle. But also deep down I knew I was not actually a 'miserable sinner' because He loved me despite that. I also began to see my family, the church and its members in a different way. Then, quite unexpectedly, I began to be aware that maybe God was calling me out for something more specific in terms of life and ministry than my present involvement with the church, which by now had become a safe and quantifiable environment. Around this time I was given a new language for prayer. It started without my being terribly conscious of it, while I was alone, driving the car one day. I opened my mouth and found myself making unimaginable sounds, but aware that in it I was both laughing, and praising God. I remember glancing at myself in the rear view mirror and stopping short, saying, 'Is this really me?' It was a gift I felt self-conscious about at first, but it became a regular part of my time with the Lord, especially with my Bible open early in the morning, when my sleepy mind was still trying to get to grips with the day. From that first time I have never been at a loss for prayer during the enormous amount of time one seems to spend in cars nowadays.

I anguished over where life was going from here. For a long time I hid it from my wife. She had come to a living faith even more recently than I had, and our ability to cope with the changes and challenges which were going on in us as individuals, let alone in our life together, was often less than adequate. The blame, I know, was attributable to me, seeking to force the pace, and Sue felt she was being dragged down paths along which she did not want to go. Sadly, our church was unable to pastor us, for to most people, most of the time, we seemed to have 'got it together'. But the Lord was gracious, and we came out stronger for what we yet had to work through.

As the conviction of a calling on my life became stronger, I began to panic. I had a good job, prospects, a nice home; and what about the family? But what was pressing on my heart was also being reflected and affirmed back at me by people around me, many of whom did not have a clue what was going on inside me or the effect of what they had said. It was not all that long, of course, before Sue was aware and it came out on to the table.

'Well, you'd better knock on a few doors,'she said. 'And if they're closed, then we'll be clear what the answer is.' Only much later did she admit that that was what she was hoping would happen. Remarkably, when it was finally confirmed that I was to go forward for ordination training, we were at peace about it together, praise God.

There followed a year when, in a sense, we were in limbo. In my spiritual life, however, it was to be a year which has probably had more effect on my formation than any other.

A new vicar arrived in our parish, and my eyes were opened to an understanding of the God of the Bible who was also God of today. Suddenly, instead of unmemorable moral dissertations, the Word of God from the pulpit came alive. But more particularly we learned that God intervenes, convicts, heals, reconciles and anoints. This was the first year that John Wimber came to the UK, and our vicar came back on fire from his conference. Not only was God doing it in the church around me, a lot was happening inside me as well.

I met Wimber myself some two years later at Acts 86, and there is no doubt that these two men—one famous, one quite shy and self-effacing—have been major instruments in forming the platform of my theology today.

I now want to jump ahead several years, not because the intervening period was uneventful, but because there is perhaps less to say about my spiritual development. I passed through theological college and four years in a curacy in Reading. It would not be true to say that I did not move spiritually during those times; indeed I believe I moved a lot, such were the challenges and buffeting of academic theology, of many pastoral situations, of my parochial circumstances, which were difficult, and my personal circumstances. For it was during this time that Sue was first diagnosed with breast cancer.

She responded well to treatment, and was back at work in a matter of months. Deep down we both knew that, statistically, there was a possibility we might not have finished with it, though many cancers are cured today. We both worked 'in the business' at a hospice, Sue as a senior staff nurse and myself as a part-time chaplain. What was God doing with us, and why? The answer is, of course, that He gives us only one step at a time.

From the summer of 1990 I was seeking to move to a new post. I had a restlessness for a new vision and purpose. A number of possibilities came and went. Then, out of the blue, there was a telephone call from a team rector in Wiltshire. Wiltshire? Where's that, other than Stonehenge and the A303? He had seen my c.v. and the word 'charismatic' had intrigued him enough to call me. He knew that my experience and predisposition was towards urban situations, but would I hear him out?

The post under discussion was as a team vicar responsible for two villages, one larger than the other. Three clergy, including himself, served the area of the team ministry as a whole. 'Talk about it with the last man who worked there', he said. 'He lives just down the road from you in Reading.' Bells were beginning to ring as I recalled hazy details of this newcomer to Reading. But, unlike some other posts I had enquired about, he must be pretty confident to open himself and the parishes up to a report from the previous occupant.

As we came up out of Hungerford and dropped over the ridge and into the Vale of Pewsey, we entered into a picture postcard landscape.

'You will be shown something beyond your wildest dreams', had been prophesied over us at Spring Harvest some weeks before, when we had asked for guidance as to where we were meant to be going. We met my prospective boss and his wife; it was plain we could work and pray together. Yet I was still in the middle of interviews for something else. What was right?

On the journey home, unknown to me, Sue was praying. It was a beautiful sunny May evening, and her request was impossible. She asked God for a rainbow. There were multicoloured hot air balloons drifting across the skyline: was it there? We passed a DIY supermarket, with its trade logo on a hoarding outside: no, it was not a complete rainbow. We arrived back home and, emotionally as well as physically exhausted, we sought to clear our minds and get on with other things. The next morning a young friend of ours, a nurse, came in for a cup of coffee, weary after a night of Marie Curie work with a patient who was terminally ill at home. 'You look tired,' we said, 'were you on the go all night?'

'No,' she replied, 'but I spent a lot of the time thinking of you and your interview. Every time I started dozing off, I fell to dreaming of rainbows, and then woke up with a start, feeling I had to tell you about it!'

We arrived in Burbage in August 1991. In that first year I came to wonder what I had taken on. The conservative one of the two villages seemed more conservative than I had been led to believe. I came back from meetings there feeling bruised and demoralised. The supposedly 'renewed' church in Burbage seemed to be miles further back than the church I had just left which would have made no such claim. The congregation seemed to be divided roughly into three parts. There were 'old' villagers (in the indigenous or cultural sense) who, in their approach to God, were looking for affirmation of all those values which, with those perspectives that mellow with history, seemed to epitomise the essential continuity of the rural parish. They expected me to take tea with them and their friends who did not come to church, several times a year, and to present choral mattins with a robed choir and dozens filling the pews. Then there were the rugged evangelicals, some converted through my predecessor, whose main objective in hearing the Word seemed to be to see the flaws in my interpretation of it and, as they were converted, it must be for someone else; anyway, was I 'kosher' after all —for I seemed to like candles? There was a third group who wanted renewal, and were expecting action—healings, manifestations, fireworks—and I seemed to be putting the brakes on. I could not win with any of them—let alone the individuals here and there who had axes to grind, ambitions to fulfil, status to be recognized, none of which they felt I gave justice to. Oh—and another phenomenon of rural ministry which is quite different from urban ministry: 'the village'—meaning the twelve hundred or so souls who never come to the church except for weddings and funerals, but see it as theirs and have an ever hyper-critical eye on what goes on there.

'I don't come, now you've done away with mattins.'

Me? I had nothing to do with it, and records suggest that average congregations were down to less than a dozen some ten years ago when that decision was taken.

'I am not into happy-clappy, that's not the proper way to worship God.'

Once a month we had a family service with a children's 'orchestra' of about a dozen, mainly recorder players. If you try to encourage the children, you are accused of neglecting the old. If you have a serious marriage or baptism policy, you prompt letters to the bishop. Then you are too rigid. If you do not, then you are too liberal. If you do not go to the pub you are seen as puritan and 'stand-offish'. If you do, you are seen as a boozer, and decadent. Explain and share your ideas with a few people you think might grasp them and you are 'cliquey'. If you proclaim it all from the pulpit, they say they don't understand what you are driving at or, worse than that, you are dangerous. Inside or outside the church, the expectation was that I was to be radical, progressive and engaged, without changing a thing!

It was about three months into my ministry. From the time of my arrival in these villages, it was a new experience to be celebrating, week by week, Book of Common Prayer communion services. I became aware of a strange phenomenon: that I actually found these services more worshipful than the looser form of morning worship attended by the newer generation later in the morning. About half past eight at Burbage one Sunday morning, the Lord revealed it to me quite clearly; happily the click in my thought processes was too quick for there to be any pause in Cranmer's interminable prose. The difference between the two services was this: for all its weaknesses, the eight o'clock congregation was truly seeking to worship and be 'the church'; whereas for the eleven o'clock congregation their gathering was only one amongst many, largely together because that was the 'Christian' thing to do on a Sunday. The reality of their spiritual focus was on junior church activities, house groups, study groups, men's groups, or whatever. About the same time, the Lord gave me a vision—which was quite simple. It was an enormous umbrella. I remember it, like the multi-coloured logo of a well-known insurance company. The task I was being given was to draw the people under the umbrella. The umbrella represented God's blessing, and what I understood very clearly was that my part was to build the Body; that together under the umbrella blessing would come; outside the umbrella, as individuals, we were outside His blessing.

I shared this with the congregation the following Sunday. I then knew that this meant confronting a task of breaking down as well as building up. Whatever God was proposing to do with us, I knew it could not just be tacked on to what we were doing, but needed new starts in a number of directions. I went on talking about my 'vision', for I needed to know whether the church affirmed it and owned it, or maybe I was out on a limb. I tried to encourage the idea that we had a collective discipleship as well as an individual one; a responsibility for the whole and toward each other as well as for ourselves. I was sat on very heavily by someone at one stage for using the expression 'corporate vision'. I did not actually feel that I—or my vision—was particularly radical, but it did seem to take a long time for some of this to get through. I went through significant troughs of self-doubt as to whether I had got this right and, if so, why my communication gifts were so poor that nothing apparently was happening.

My two major 'crimes' were to close down the house groups and a Saturday evening prayer group. Actually I did neither, but I was extremely concerned as to where they were going, and made it clear that I was not sure what they were doing for the Body of Christ as a whole. By this time I knew clearly that my one track objective under God during my time in Burbage was to build up the Body. Engineered change was necessary to rekindle a dynamic. The reality to me was the urgency of drawing together a wide range of individuals, some loosely grouped together for safety or comfort, into at least a 'common denominator' of teaching, understanding and agenda.

To do this I introduced the Anglican Renewal Ministries basics course entitled *Saints Alive*. There was a fair amount of resistance: 'Why do we need to do a Christian basics course?' was one of the most common comments. There were one or two, including my administrator and lay reader, who were suspicious, muttering about 'bad experiences' elsewhere. There were others who were enthused, and eagerly waiting to join a course. I put groups together by personal invitation, deliberately seeking to have a balance of personalities, ages, sexes, and drawing them from different house groups and none, to cross-profile the church as well. The breakthrough point was towards the end of the first nine-week course, when, following two previous sessions teaching on the Holy Spirit, there was an evening simply for reflection and ministry. At the end of the course there, ready-made, was the nucleus of a new house group. Undramatically, over a period of time, I was aware that the mood was shifting, increasingly. I was conscious we seemed to be closer to being on the same wavelength; that there was a new desire and expectancy of what God might do in our midst. What was He going to do?

In May 1992 Sue had a recurrence of the cancer. Being human beings, since 1989 we had sought to shut it out of our minds.The surgery was satisfactory; the chemotherapy completed with side-effects only of queasiness and tiredness. Sue was back at her work as a community nurse. Everything had returned to 'normal'. But tacitly we just knew that things were not normal. We had a good twelve months, including realizing a long harboured dream of buying ourselves a bolt-hole far enough away to escape there on days off and holidays. The children were doing well and life both in the church and the home seemed to be picking up comfortably.

Then the next blow. Mike Hanson, my lay reader and parish administrator, had been my closest confidant for the first two years of my ministry. We did not always agree, but he was intensely loyal, and often sought to mediate or 'sell' my ideas, even when he was not fully convinced himself. Above all he had time, for he had retired from business with chronic heart disease some years earlier. His wife Liz stopped outside the church early one morning, walking the dog, deeply worried. Mike felt seedy and was undergoing tests for abdominal pain; she feared the worst. It was untreatable liver cancer. In a month he was dead. It was the first of two funerals within twelve months where around four hundred people sang, *Lord, the light of your love is shining*, at the top of their voices.

About the same time as Mike's death, Sue developed a tickly cough. Various treatments from our doctor had no effect and the cough continued. Asthma was suggested. Two weeks later came her regular check-up with the breast clinic, when the cough was discussed. At the next appointment, a bleak five minute interview warned us of the worst. Two weeks later, tests confirmed it; I remember the two of us sitting in the car, blankly staring at a brick wall. We had nothing to say.

It was three months before Sue died. Thank God, until the last twenty four hours or so it was not even painful or distressing—as an illness; just the heartache of watching our lives slipping apart while desperately trying to hold on to the togetherness. I shouted at God and became very selfish: why were we being cheated, just at a point when things were coming together? What about our family life—the children, the grandchildren we would never enjoy together? Why us? Why me? Thirty years of life just down the drain.

I wondered whether God had somehow withdrawn His favour from us. In my own numbness I was totally inadequate for months. There was my grief, and that of the children, to work through. I felt drained physically, mentally, emotionally and spiritually. I could not feel a sense of God's presence; often I could not feel myself; I was living as a kind of automaton, going through the motions, detached from the import of what I was saying from the pulpit or trying to get to grips with in the parish.

People were very kind to us in this period; after all they were hurting too, both for us and for themselves. Inevitably, though, for some time I tended to hide behind my new parish administrator, Barry Smith, and emotionally I leant upon those who understood—my mother, who had now lost two children in law, as well as two of her own, and her husband; my daughter Naomi who was at home with me, and Liz Hanson, who herself had been widowed scarcely a year at this stage.

For the church at Burbage it was a year of retrenchment, but it was also a year of finding new vision. I use the word 'find' rather than 'seek' for it was a process of discovery that far from forsaking us, God was with us all the time, and was gradually preparing us for a new phase in the building of His kingdom. I do believe it was this passive receptivity rather than energetic activism (which I was unable to apply anyway), that enabled us to hear, discern and take on board amongst the many voices there always are, what He actually wanted for us. The clearest voice was His love could not insulate us from the fallen world, including sickness and death, but *was* all-powerful, and had overcome them.

The first vehicle of change was the unlikely one of a Lent course prescribed for the diocese and written by our Bishop. When it was first mentioned, in the autumn after Sue died, it was one more thing I allowed to go over my head. It was to my embarrassment that at a late stage I realised that if we did not do it as a parish we would be odd ones out in the Diocese. By this stage it was too late to set it up as a Lent programme. The solution was to fit it into the weeks after Easter, leading up to Ascensiontide and Pentecost, and we closed all the house groups meeting during that period.

The course consisted of a message from the Bishop on tape for each week; we then divided into groups to discuss it, had a cup of tea, and went home. The recommendation was that we start with worship; specifically, the latest liturgy for common prayer, devised by the Bishop himself. With respect to the Bishop, I knew we would never get past the first week if I subjected our congregation to that, so with a guitar, subsequently added to with keyboard and drums, we started these meetings with twenty minutes or so of informal praise. Thus was born a monthly meeting, which continues to this day and has become a major focus for renewal, teaching and ministry in the Holy Spirit. Through the teaching, it also provides the theme and keynote for the house group Bible studies for the remainder of each month, which I put together myself and are therefore common ground for the major part of the church at any time.

The second vehicle for change was my parish administrator. Barry was a man with enormous energy and organisational ability, who read all the latest books. He had the right language and an impressive range of the right churchy contacts. I depended on him enormously. But where was he in his relationship with Jesus? I saw in him so much of myself only a few years back, before I was converted, striving so hard after what he admired in others, yet afraid to really jump in and risk himself— all this with a kind of charismatic overcoat on it. Then, out of the blue, I found he and his wife Liz had booked themselves to go to Toronto, to visit what was then the Airport Vineyard Church (the 'Toronto Blessing' was about six months into its heyday). Liz! The supreme sceptic who only felt safe at family services where she could tell herself that the sermon was for the children! I couldn't believe it! Then I was jealous that they didn't offer to take me with them—though I suspect that if they had, it might have been a different story. Liz was converted and they both came back in overdrive.

The third vehicle for change was *Alpha*, which had by this time been taken up with enthusiasm by the Christian press. But again, with the day to day pressures of simply rebuilding my life, let alone the parish, I had allowed it to pass me by. It was something which, with his new found zeal, Barry had got his teeth into. He had thoroughly enjoyed a course put on by the Harnhill Centre for Christian Healing, near Cirencester, with which our church, and he in particular, had had long-standing links. I was less than enthusiastic, mainly because the obvious immediate market would be all those whom I had scarcely a year before completed processing through the *Saints Alive* material. How could I subject them to another basics course? Was this really what God wanted? Did I get it all wrong in what I had gone through before?

The issue came to a head in the autumn. Barry had been drafted into a group planning a deanery-wide mission for the following year—he had been infecting the others with his enthusiasm and it was decided to hold an Alpha course for leaders of all the deanery churches. The course was relaxed and informal, hosted by a local farmer in his home. I am not sure what it did for the others who were there but, yes, I could see its potential and so gave Barry the go-ahead to get a group together to run one in Burbage after Christmas.

The fourth vehicle for change was strictly personal, but profound indeed for us all. Over the year, Liz Hanson and I had been getting closer and closer. We put it first to our children, then to my bishop and finally to the church that we wanted to get married. When we told the four children, they burst out laughing because they had been taking bets behind our backs as to when it would happen. My bishop was delighted, and he agreed a date there and then to conduct the service. When we told the church there was spontaneous applause, and immense joy and happiness for us.

We did feel powerfully that God's hand was in it. The passage from the Bible which came to mind was the story of Ruth being redeemed by her late husband's kinsman Boaz. It did seem so right for us, for the church; and for our four children—for though by now they were young adults, it gave a sense of security and stability for their one remaining parent. Even amongst the secular community there was a sense that it was right, and over five hundred came to the wedding.

For our honeymoon we fulfilled a long-held ambition for both of us to go to the Canadian Rockies. It was beautiful. On the last weekend we were in Toronto and visited the Airport Church. I have to say that, no, neither of us collapsed in a heap on the floor. We discovered on our return that there were those who felt disappointed that we had not done so, but the Spirit works gently as well as in wind and fire and, after all we had been through, we possibly did not need any more breaking down, but rather building up, renewal of confidence, and encouragement in our life and calling together. We did come back to England with a sense of common identity in the Lord, a real awareness that He was blessing us for the work that there was to do—oh, and we found that we could pray together.

In February 1996 I went with Barry to a conference in Bournemouth, entitled *Waves of the Spirit*. I did not feel any particular need to go, but I usually try to get to some outside event most years. This one was convenient, because we could travel to it daily, and it was being hosted by Peter Lawrence whom I knew, with a number of good names on the 'cast list'. In the event, we nearly abandoned our attendance; it was the worst week's weather for years, with snowfalls, fog and ice all through the week.

We reached the fourth day of the conference, which was making no impact on me up to that point, though it had been enjoyable. In the afternoon there appeared on stage someone I had never come across before, to whom I took an instant dislike. He was a Canadian church leader, and he came over to me as the worst kind of caricature 'tele-evangelist'—strident, pretentious, name-dropping; everything he delivered he shouted at such a furious pace and with such a thick accent we could scarcely follow him, and all this he did whilst strutting up and down from one end of the stage to the other, only pausing, it seemed, when he wanted to be sure we had caught one of his funny lines. He went on, and on, and on—so frequently repeating himself that even I got the gist of his story after a while.

Basically, he was giving his testimony—his testimony of re-conviction by the Holy Spirit concerning his calling and ministry as a pastor and evangelist. What came over again and again was how he felt consumed from within by what he described as 'holy fire,' which had to come out. I had to go forward for ministry.

I was very quiet on the way home that night, but I knew the same thing was happening to me. Maybe a spark ignited in Toronto was coming to life, maybe this was quite independent of that; it is not important which. 'What should I do?' I asked Barry, 'I have already prepared my sermon for Sunday.'

The Sunday service passed as far as the third hymn, but there seemed to be a sense of expectancy as they all sat down. Simply, I repeated what I had heard on the Thursday, and described what was happening to me. Then, without any hype or exhortation I finished by saying that if anyone wanted some of that 'holy fire', would they like to come up to receive prayer for it. What if no-one came forward? This is a village church! Barry came up for prayer. (He told me afterwards that he made a move because he felt sorry for me.) I prayed simply that he, too, would receive this 'holy fire' as he stood there with his back to the congregation and his eyes shut.

'Barry,' I said, 'you'd better help me with praying.'

'What for?' he thought, but what he could not see was that nearly half the church was pounding up the aisle behind him.

I remember little of the next half hour, except my own incredulity at what was happening around us as the Spirit took over, with only the simplest of prayer invitations on our part. There were bodies all over the chancel, with an age range of sixteen to eighty-six. There were lone figures, with half-smiles and glazed looks, lolling in pews. People were laughing, crying, hugging each other with feeling, some for the first time in their lives. There were others just quietly mouthing praises to God. One dominant thought in my mind was quite unspiritual: we must do something about shifting these choirstalls!

By the middle of the next week the doubts had set in. Will there be a reaction? What would anybody have thought if they had come in from outside just then? What about the village? What would the bishop think? And the Lord said, 'Go and tell him.' The bishop was enormously encouraging and supportive, and only gave me some wise advice about the kind of parameters we should set ourselves and guidelines for ministry.

It did not happen again, but then God is not into performances, and that manifestation of His power and presence amongst us all was what we plainly needed. I would like to say that from that point we have not looked back, but this would be both trite and untrue. However, from that point there was a new sense of purpose and dynamism. Not just as individuals, or as little in-groups of a particular kind, but *together* as a pretty comprehensive gathering of God's people on a Sunday morning, we had seen the reality of God. The old 'vision' of the umbrella and God's blessing on His people in their togetherness, was actually taking substance as the Spirit worked amongst us. There were new convictions and conversions, and reconciliations. Our first *Alpha* Holy Spirit day approached with a whole new expectation from what it might have been only a few weeks back: we were not disappointed. In the first year or two following that February 'blessing' the church seemed to grow in every direction. Yes, we started to grow in numbers: significantly through *Alpha*, where there have been some exciting conversions and coming to life in the Spirit. (At the time of writing we are about to start our seventh course.) But others through the Holy Spirit have been renewed in their conviction and commitment to Christ. Yet others have simply come through the doors and felt God here, whether they have immediately recognized that or not. There has been a different sense of purpose and identity in the house groups, not least because of the focal point of the monthly midweek meeting. Worship has taken on a new quality and depth. Junior church numbers are rising again, having been falling for some time. There are four small but flourishing prayer groups that meet every week, with a co-ordinator who provides material in the form of a weekly 'prayer watch', identifying needs and updating notice boards. The PCC have regular 'awaydays' for study and reflection. We have renewal days, with gifted outside speakers attracting numbers from far afield. We held a parish weekend this last year attended by over fifty, and we have another one planned. Ministry in the Holy Spirit is a part of every meeting or service where I am (or another priest is) present, administered by a team of trained ministers. We now have a counselling co-ordinator, for those who need more in-depth care.

We have attracted a measure of notice outside. A number of individuals and groups from our church have been asked to help with events at other churches, both in our own Salisbury Diocese and elsewhere. Some of us are expected to provide input to diocesan planning and events. During a four day visit to the diocese two years ago, the Archbishop of Canterbury included a visit to hear first hand of our experiences of renewal.

There are of course problems with being a 'successful' church. The first is in the word 'successful' itself, which in its painful subjectivity is both a snare to vanity and open to the most wild and dangerous interpretation. Churches are obsessed with the numbers game; it has been well said that small churches are not just failed large churches, but for the kind of church we are, or seem to be becoming, most outsiders tend to think of suburban models with 'wall to wall' congregations. We are actually some one hundred and fifty in regular membership.

'Success' also can attract an eclectic following, some of whom have a great deal to give, but which can sour relations with churches whence they come. There will be others who come for the wrong reasons, full of resentments and disappointments from elsewhere, and unrealistic expectations in a place God has not brought them to. There are also detractors, who have been part of the history but not carried with it. Some of these may talk the church down within its walls, which may be demoralising but is at least challengeable; more damaging are those who do so outside, among already sceptical secular groups within the community. It is almost as though there are some who would be happier if the church were empty but for a few old ladies and a Rowan Atkinson caricature of a vicar. There is a widespread belief that we are swinging from the chandeliers every time we meet—would that we were! 'Happy-clappy' is the ultimate expression of disdain, though I cannot recall an occasion when the congregation have indulged in orchestrated clapping since I have been here, other than at the midweek parents and toddlers service.

Where are we now? One of my main concerns in this last year has been the easy drift into routine and complacency—I preached one Sunday morning recently against 'a spirit of sogginess' which I saw upon the church. Repentance has been a major recurring theme on my mind, not so much of specific misdemeanours, but essentially of attitudes, values, and general laziness—taking things for granted. Sadly that is so easy, even when God's love and the com-passion—the 'suffering with'—of Jesus has been so poignant and heart-warming in our experience, without which we would never have got to this point of testimony. The Spirit is still working among us, sometimes with a shock to some old lags, as folk who have come from nowhere cruise past as if they were supercharged. But, as Mike Pilavachi of Soul Survivor said recently, 'Perhaps we are, so to speak, in a "lull" between one "wave" of the Spirit and the next.' The important thing is that we should see that too as an opportunity—to prepare ourselves for the next deluge of God's power, and the purpose for which He might bring it. To Him alone be the glory.

A Heart for Jesus

BOB PITCHER

Vicar of Caereithin, Swansea,
Anglican Chaplain for Cefn Coed Mental Hospital
and National Chaplain for 'Faith and Light'

In 1965, becoming a vicar could not have been further from my mind. After all I was playing keyboard and blues harp full time with 'The Betterdays', a West Country Rhythm and Blues phenomenon. We were being dragged off the stage by fans, and the *New Musical Express* had said that we made the Rolling Stones sound like the Monkees! I don't know whether the acclaim was deserved, but certainly I was out to live as wildly as I could and an 'R & B' band seemed the best way of doing that. From the age of eleven I had understood that I had a heart condition which was unlikely to sustain life beyond my mid-twenties, so I was eating, drinking and being merry for all I was worth. The Congregational church which I had attended with my anxious parents since the age of six had never shown me a 'life grabbing' Jesus—or, if it had, I was too preoccupied to notice. So, with this grating time-bomb in my chest, I was hell-bent on squeezing as much selfish pleasure as I could from the swinging sixties.

Unsurprisingly, therefore, at my annual check up at the Bristol General in 1965, when I was eighteen years old, the cardiologist announced that my heart was becoming enlarged and they needed to act. I was not one of your normal 'hole in the hearts' which were being routinely repaired by then; but, being an awkward customer, I was also the proud owner of two faulty valves which, for some reason, complicated the surgery. To be honest, the thought of open heart surgery—on a condition that I knew was difficult—filled me with terror. During my early teens I had lain for hours on examination tables whilst some of the best brains around had argued about the possibility of my surviving the knife. I was tempted to believe that I was some sort of guinea pig. On top of this, they had not told me whether the one other bloke with my particular problem had survived his 'job'. So I knew this was a risky business and, as a free-spirited teenager, I was just not ready for it. It has to be admitted, however, that 'free-spirited' was not an accurate description of my state. I was in fact as spiritually bound up as a trussed chicken, had I but known it.

Well, the great 'open heart' day arrived. I literally said goodbye to the world with a scrap of paper, on which I scrawled a poem about going into a dark wood and being left behind. Leaving this literary offering for posterity beside my glass of pink stuff on the bed side unit, I submitted myself fatefully to the surgeon, really thinking that was it. Little did I know that it was going to be the beginning of a new adventure.

I will never know for sure what happened during the operation. The surgeon said that I had died for a short while. After being repaired, my heart decided that it quite liked resting, following all the strain of living in a rock and roll musician—so for some time it refused to start again. Eventually it did. Soon afterwards, its proud owner woke up with it, but to a very different world. Things had profoundly changed. Over the next day or so, several things dawned on me which before had never been more than academic possibilities. Through a great deal of confusion, and some bodily weakness, I began to realize that God was real. Not real as a concept, but as the one in whom we 'live, move and have our very being'. I was the goldfish. He was the water. 'Well,' you say, 'that must have been wonderful!' Actually it was terrifying, because I was not at peace with Him. For the first time in my life I knew (how I knew I don't know) that I was answerable for my life—and that I had no answers for it. I went over and over my past; and all the selfishness and sheer grot of it was a horrible cesspit. I felt as if I had totally wasted my life. This was compounded by a sort of 'out of body experience' a few days after the operation, which had more than a passing similarity to some Biblical descriptions of hell. These experiences caused me to make two serious decisions. Firstly, to get right with God. Somehow or other I had to make amends and get back into God's 'good books' (if I had ever been there in the first place.) Secondly, I wanted to give my life to serving Him. I was amazed that I had never thought of that before.

Physically, I started getting better, and this was such a relief. The operation had been a limited success, certainly enough of a success to extend my life to something like a normal span. So now I had a chance to find God and serve Him. But who was He? I wasn't even sure that

He was Jesus. But now there was an open road of discovery ahead. Surely it would lead to some answers.

As a result of this change I was quite a different animal returning home to my bemused parents. I discovered where the kitchen was and washed up the odd cup and saucer. Rock musician expletives were removed from my vocabulary and I even started to pray and read my Bible. Every old and infirm person in the area was visited (whether they wanted me or not.) All this I did in my attempt to become a Christian. By that time I had a pretty good idea that Jesus was probably quite central to my search, but I really thought I had to impress him with my changed life style and vigorous attempts to be good. All my efforts were in vain though. No matter how hard I tried to be like a Christian, I couldn't get any Peace. The 'cesspit' followed me everywhere. It was a stinking reminder of my past that just would not go away. My liberal, church-going friends looked on helplessly.

Having been brought up a good liberal, it was with some distaste that I now decided to go along to the definitely evangelical Christian Union at the Plymouth Tech. In my effort to become a Christian I had decided to become a teacher, for which I needed 'A' levels, and Plymouth Technical College was the place to get them. I went along to the C.U.

My worst fears were confirmed. They really did speak in Elizabethan English (Elizabeth I, that is) and they dressed as if clothes rationing was still in operation. But they did have the answer. Despite all their quaint ways and words, they had what I was looking for. In many ways they were normal, screwed-up students, stressed about deadlines and exams—except that God was visibly with them. My first inkling was the way they prayed. I had heard many, many people saying prayers over the years, but these students were the first people I had heard praying. They were actually talking to God as if He could hear, understand and do something. It was all part of a package. They believed that God was involved in every part of their perfectly normal lives (perfectly normal, apart from their 1960s evangelical idiosyncrasies, that is.) I could see the reality of it. It created some hope in me and I desperately wanted what they had. But the question was, 'How can I get it?' Was it available to me? Or had I completely blown it for ever, with my reckless excesses as a would-be pop star? So, as I went through the motions of doing 'A' level English and Sociology, I became the plague of the Tech. C.U., asking questions at every opportunity. 'How do you know your sins are forgiven? How do you know you are going to Heaven? What is the unforgivable sin?' I would even sit by students in the library, who were desperately trying to do revision for their finals, and try to get answers. Every speaker at the C.U. meetings got a barrage of questions from me. I must pay tribute to the longsuffering members of the group, who patiently tried to get me to understand the Gospel. Sadly, however, the penny didn't seem to drop for me. I tried harder and harder to find this elusive Peace and Forgiveness. My kind friends seemed to be telling me that before I could be effective as a Christian, or even call myself a Christian at all, I had to receive something from God. Jesus, they told me, had died for my sins, however bad I thought they were, and I had to receive forgiveness as a gift. My desire to serve Him was not in question, but my ability, or perhaps willingness, to receive from Him was. For me it all sounded so trite, so 'old hat'. Surely, I thought, there must be some great spiritual 'thing' that I should accomplish, some pilgrimage or intense trial I should go through. Inwardly, though, I was becoming increasingly weary of the cesspit of my past, and the worry of what might happen to me if I died as I was. So finally, in February 1967, almost a year after this adventure had begun, I threw in the towel. Kneeling beside my bed, I prayed a prayer that I had seen on the back of Victory Tracts....I think. It was something like this,

Dear Lord Jesus, I know that I'm a sinner.
Thank you for dying on the cross for my sins.
Please forgive me for my sins.
Please come into my heart and be my Lord and Saviour.
I thank you for doing it. Amen.

Almost immediately, I was overwhelmed by Love and Power. For some reason, I shook like a leaf. Waves of pure joy flowed through the whole of my being. The 'cesspit' was expelled from me, and I knew myself to be as clean as the driven snow. The overwhelming darkness of guilt and shame was gone, and I now possessed a deep knowledge that God loved me and that I was accepted by Him. How long that ecstasy continued I cannot tell, only that eventually I rolled into bed and asked God if I might die. It seemed to me a good idea at the time, since at last I knew that I was OK with Him. Besides, it was the only way I could think of in which to get any closer. God did not grant that prayer however, but the main thing was that I had at last found the object of my searching... or had He found me? A new life had begun.

Another thing which is worth recording occurred that night. Almost as a bonus, I began to speak in a new language: the gift of tongues. In my theologically 'topsy turvy' way I had been wanting this gift. After having met a group of young Pentecostals who impressed me very much I had also wanted what they had. They were like the college C.U. lot, but even more so. They had an enthusiasm and vivacity in their Christian life which was infectious. They attributed this 'fire' to the 'Baptism in the Holy Spirit'. Each one of them claimed to have a dateable experience of receiving it. They believed that this 'enduing with power' was always accompanied by speaking in tongues (not a view that I now share). So I was looking for that as well. I did not know whether there was a particular order for getting these things, but I was out for all I could get and so seemed to receive it all as a sort of package.

For eighteen months after that experience I floated through life on a cloud and was probably of little use to man or God, but it was a very healing time. I discovered that worship could be, and often is, life's greatest joy. I found that God would actually guide me. I was very bad at that at first, and had the reputation for being 'fearfully and wonderfully led'. But I knew He was doing it. I began to discover my new family the Church, and had wonderful experiences of being part of a loving and affirming community of faith. Conversion had been a truly radical experience and all things did 'become new'. I suppose that because of my lack of awareness of difficulties over what have become known as the 'gifts of the Spirit' I found myself a natural Pentecostal; then in time I became a leader in the 'house church' movement. It was not until I reached middle age that I found myself being drawn towards the beautiful liturgy and stabilizing tradition of Anglicanism.

Then, to my greatest surprise (and that of the Director of Ordinands), there came the growing conviction that I was actually being called into ordained ministry within the Anglican Church. But how was an ex-rock musician, and 'house-church' elder going to fit into parish ministry? I have to say that there were some who said that I could not and would not. My kind and affirming bishop in the Salisbury Diocese, however, felt that the things which I had learnt from my chequered past were actually worthwhile gifts to bring with me into the Church of England. So Salisbury kindly sent me to Trinity College Bristol. Somehow, though, I ended up in the Church in Wales, who equally kindly repaid

Salisbury for my training! In 1992 I was ordained in the Swansea and Brecon Diocese. The question still remained, how was I to fit in? I was, of course, aware of many Anglican churches which had embarked on the adventurous journey that included the kind of worship and Holy Spirit involvement which I had grown used to. I was aware that as well as excitement and discovery there could be pain and alienation. One of the biggest challenges ahead seemed to be enabling church members to grasp the idea that God Himself wanted to be involved in our lives individually and corporately. It was challenging to create an expectation that, in our services, God, through His Holy Spirit, would be there in a way that we could engage with and, as a result, He might even do things that we had not planned. His presence might be tangibly experienced; He might want us to sing things that were not on the list. He might draw people into a relationship with Himself. He might even heal people. It appeared to me that in many of our Anglican churches we had learned how to 'do' church beautifully, but had lost the expectation that God Himself might show up. So, as I began to preach this idea, some of these things began to occur. Inevitably this produced a number of reactions. Some of course were angry that I had implied that change was necessary and that the calm of predictable and well ordered services was being interrupted by 'happenings'. Others were fearful of where it might lead, but went along with it. But there were also those who realized that this was what they had been looking for, some for many years, and who embraced the 'Good News' wholeheartedly. I began to introduce 'renewal style' worship songs which gave expression to, and in some cases fanned into life, a new longing of heart.

We also began praying for people during services by the 'laying on of hands'. Some of the results were dramatic; like the lovely nurse who said that her dead-heart had been brought back to life, by Jesus. Several years earlier, her young son had tragically died. This caused her to die emotionally, but now she is able to feel, to love, and laugh normally again. And there was the woman who was healed from the imprisonment of serious agoraphobia and obesity, after prayer and anointing with oil at 'home communion'. God has enabled her to become an outgoing, socially active and attractively slim young lady. But I suppose the greatest miracle, though, has been a community of people, one by one, becoming God-conscious and God-expectant.

My parish is one of the most socially deprived areas in Wales.

Unemployment, drug and alcohol abuse, crime and violence abound. At heart, though, it is a lovely, but hurting community of 'down to earth' people. As a result of my experiences I know that the answer lies with individuals coming into a living relationship with God through Christ and knowing the power of the Holy Spirit in their lives, whether their experience of this is a radical 'about turn' like mine or a gentler process of entering into new life. But in order to make Jesus accessible, we have needed to try and find new ways of being 'Anglican'. For instance in an area, like ours, where literacy skills are limited, people have been terrified by being handed three books and a bulletin at the door. We speak in a language which is highly specialized and, frankly, esoteric. I have seen people reach for their money when the 'collect' is announced! There are so many 'hoops' through which we ask people to jump before they can even begin to get a glimpse of Jesus! We have needed to be adventurous (but still Anglican) with our services, and as a community we are needing to develop welcoming and accepting hearts. I remember, in my 'Rock' days longing to belong, somewhere, anywhere; to be acceptable and accepted: to be valued and affirmed. So I believe that one of the greatest things the Holy Spirit is doing to-day is to build communities of faith which extend that kind of accepting love to those who have found very little love in life. We are beginning to see the 'unloved' drawn to our community and, through this, to Christ. I was an outcast, whom Jesus called to himself. I trust that through my ministry more and more outcasts will come to know that they too are 'special' to him.

And the Rock Music? Well you ought to hear our Evensongs!

For he is the living God and he endures forever;
his kingdom will not be destroyed,
his dominion will never end.
He rescues and he saves;
he performs signs and wonders
in the heavens and on the earth.

Daniel 6:26b–27a

BOOKS BY PETER H. LAWRENCE

DOING WHAT COMES SUPERNATURALLY
Learning how to minister in the power of the Holy Spirit
Extremely useful for ministers and church members who
want to learn more about ministering—includes sound
biblical teaching on healing and deliverance.
ISBN 0952268841   £5.99

THE HOT LINE
How can we hear God speak—today?
Preface by Michael Green
Foreword by David Pytches
A parish church moves into renewal. People begin to hear
words from the Lord. How do we discern what is from God?
This classic account is described by the author
as 'a beginner's book, written by a beginner for beginners.'
ISBN 0952268868   £5.99

CHRISTIAN HEALING
A thoroughly biblical and practical approach. How Jesus
healed the sick; how the disciples healed the sick; how we
can minister for healing, in the power of the Holy Spirit.
Excellent value—ideal for teaching, and for ministry teams.
ISBN 0952268876   £3.95

AVAILABLE FROM CHRISTIAN BOOKSHOPS

A new Bible-based study resource from
TERRA NOVA PUBLICATIONS

GROWING IN THE WORD:
HOW TO BECOME THE CHRISTIAN GOD WANTS YOU TO BE
By Hilary Latham   ISBN 1 901949 02 8   £5.99
This book explains twenty key themes in narrative form.

TOWARDS CHRISTIAN MATURITY COURSE MANUAL
By Hilary Latham   ISBN 0 9531494 1 2   £6.95
Packed with biblical references, and helpful explanation.
In a convenient lay-flat large ring-bound format.

The course is designed to help Christians to move in the power and love of the Holy Spirit, and to:

> **KNOW** the written word of God
> **BELIEVE** the word of God
> **RENEW THE MIND** in accordance with the word of God
> **SPEAK** in line with the word of God
> **EXERCISE** faith according to the word of God
> **PRAY** in line with the word of God
> **LEARN** to recognise the voice of God
> **MINISTER** effectively in accordance with the word of God
> **UNDERSTAND** covenant relationship with God
> **RECEIVE** the blessings which flow from obedience
> **DEAL WITH BARRIERS** to growth into maturity
> **DISCOVER THE ABUNDANT LIFE** that Jesus promised

Clear and accessible to Christians of all ages, this course is packed with relevant scripture texts. Leaders can easily adapt the materials to suit local needs. The two publications are complementary, so it is recommended, though not essential, that every participant should have a copy of each.

More good books from
TERRA NOVA PUBLICATIONS

THE STRUGGLE

THE BATTLE BETWEEN FLESH AND SPIRIT
by Hartmut Kopsch

You are not alone —every Christian is involved in
THE STRUGGLE —each day!
The power of the flesh is manifested in jealousy, pride,
gossip, grumbling, covetousness, boasting, blaming
and fear, which so often hinder the lives of individual
Christians and churches, and spoil our relationship
with God.

  In this book, the Rector of Walcot, Bath, teaches how to
apply the resources of the Holy Spirit, as we engage in
THE STRUGGLE. The author's honesty and openness
about his own struggle will help many who long to
overcome the flesh and enjoy the life of the Spirit
to the full.

ISBN 1 901949 01 X   £7.99

A FAITH THAT WORKS

by Don Latham

The author of this book has immense professional experience as
a Chief Executive. He is also a powerful and effective Christian
speaker, who shows that faith in the living God is for the whole
of life, including the workplace.

  The author describes how he was led into renewal, and a new
dependence on the Holy Spirit, following a remarkable experience
of God in Bath Abbey. The Bishop asked him to go around the
diocese teaching about finance and Christian giving. His hearers
often discovered that God was beginning to affect their lives in
unexpected ways. Don has seen many people born again, filled
with the Holy Spirit and, often, healed.

ISBN 1 901949 00 1   £6.99